Unlocking The Sharpness of Unbreakable Healthy Brain :

Proven Strategies Book for a Sharp, Resilient Brain

Table of Contents

Introduction 6
    Understanding Cognitive Health 6
    The Importance of Brain Fitness 10
    Debunking Myths About Dementia and Cognitive Decline 14

Chapter 1: Understanding the Brain 19
    Basic Brain Anatomy and Function 19
    How the Brain Ages 25
    What Causes Cognitive Decline? 31

Chapter 2: The Science of Neuroplasticity 37
    What is Neuroplasticity? 37
    How Neuroplasticity Can Reverse Damage 42
    Practical Applications of Neuroplasticity in Daily Life 48

Chapter 3: Nutrition for Brain Health 54
    Essential Nutrients for Cognitive Function 54
    The Impact of Diet on Brain Health 60
    Brain-Boosting Foods and Recipes 66

Chapter 4: Exercise and the Brain 74
    Physical Exercise and Cognitive Health 74
    Types of Exercises That Improve Brain Function 80
    Creating a Brain-Healthy Fitness Routine 87

Chapter 5: Mental Exercises and Brain Training 95
    Cognitive Exercises to Enhance Memory and Focus . 95

Puzzles, Games, and Activities for Brain Health.......102

The Role of Lifelong Learning in Cognitive Longevity 110

Chapter 6: Stress Management and Brain Health 117

The Impact of Stress on Cognitive Function 117

Mindfulness, Meditation, and Relaxation Techniques 123

Developing Resilience Against Cognitive Decline ...130

Chapter 7: Sleep and Brain Function 137

How Sleep Affects Cognitive Health 137

Tips for Improving Sleep Quality............................143

Understanding Sleep Disorders and Their Impact on the Brain 149

Chapter 8: Social Connections and Cognitive Health..156

The Role of Social Interaction in Preventing Cognitive Decline..156

Building and Maintaining Strong Social Networks.162

Activities and Communities That Promote Cognitive Engagement 170

Chapter 9: Brain Health and Technology 178

The Benefits and Risks of Technology on Cognitive Health...178

Balancing Screen Time and Cognitive Engagement185

Chapter 10: Early Signs of Cognitive Decline and What to Do 191

Recognizing the Early Signs of Cognitive Decline....191

Steps to Take When You Notice Changes 198

    Professional Help and Therapies Available 204

Chapter 11: Personalized Brain Health Plans 211

    Creating a Personalized Brain Health Action Plan..211

    Setting Goals and Tracking Progress 218

    Adapting Your Plan as You Age 224

Chapter 12: Future Directions in Brain Health..............233

    Advances in Brain Research and Treatments 233

    Promising Therapies and Interventions.....................239

    The Future of Cognitive Health and Longevity..........248

Conclusion 256

Introduction

Understanding Cognitive Health

Cognitive health refers to the state of being mentally sharp, clear, and capable of processing information efficiently. It involves several key brain functions, including memory, attention, executive function, processing speed, and language skills. These cognitive abilities are essential for everyday tasks such as remembering appointments, solving problems, making decisions, and communicating effectively.

1. Key Components of Cognitive Health:

- **Memory:** The brain's ability to store and retrieve information. This includes short-term memory (holding information temporarily) and long-term memory (storing information for extended periods).

- **Attention:** The capacity to concentrate on specific information or tasks while ignoring distractions. It plays a crucial role in learning and performing complex tasks.

- **Executive Function:** A set of higher-order cognitive processes used for planning, organizing, problem-solving, and managing time. Executive function is vital for making decisions and adapting to new situations.

- **Processing Speed:** The rate at which the brain takes in, understands, and responds to information. Faster processing speeds allow for more efficient cognitive functioning.

- **Language:** The ability to understand, process, and produce language. It encompasses skills such as reading, writing, and verbal communication.

2. Importance of Cognitive Health:

Maintaining cognitive health is critical for independence and quality of life. Cognitive decline can impact various aspects of daily living, including the ability to perform routine tasks, maintain social connections, and make informed decisions. Good cognitive health also supports emotional regulation and mental well-being, contributing to a more fulfilling and active life.

3. Factors Affecting Cognitive Health:

- **Aging:** While some cognitive changes are a normal part of aging, such as slower processing speed and occasional forgetfulness, these do not necessarily lead to significant cognitive decline.

- **Lifestyle Choices:** Diet, physical activity, sleep, and stress management all significantly impact cognitive health. Poor lifestyle choices, such as a high-fat diet, sedentary behavior, and chronic stress, can increase the risk of cognitive decline.

- **Medical Conditions:** Chronic conditions like diabetes, hypertension, depression, and heart disease can negatively impact cognitive function. Managing these conditions effectively is crucial for maintaining brain health.

- **Environmental Factors:** Exposure to toxins, pollutants, and lack of intellectual stimulation can contribute to cognitive decline. Engaging in mentally stimulating activities and maintaining a clean environment are vital for brain health.

4. Normal Aging vs. Cognitive Decline:

It's essential to differentiate between normal age-related cognitive changes and signs of cognitive decline or dementia. Normal aging may involve slower recall of names or facts but does not significantly affect daily functioning. In contrast, cognitive decline involves noticeable impairments in memory, reasoning, and decision-making that interfere with daily life.

5. Myths and Facts About Cognitive Decline:

- **Myth:** Cognitive decline is an inevitable part of aging.
    - **Fact:** While some decline in cognitive abilities may occur with age, significant impairment is not inevitable. Many older adults maintain sharp cognitive function well into their later years through healthy lifestyle choices and mental engagement.
- **Myth:** Dementia is synonymous with memory loss.
    - **Fact:** While memory loss is a common symptom of dementia, it also affects other cognitive functions such as language, problem-solving, and executive function.

Dementia is a progressive condition that goes beyond just forgetfulness.

6. Scientific Insights into Cognitive Health:

Recent research shows that the brain possesses remarkable plasticity, known as neuroplasticity, which allows it to reorganize and form new neural connections throughout life. This adaptability means that cognitive decline can be mitigated or even reversed through targeted interventions, such as cognitive training, physical exercise, and proper nutrition. Additionally, neurogenesis—the formation of new neurons—continues in certain parts of the brain, like the hippocampus, which is crucial for learning and memory.

7. Strategies for Maintaining Cognitive Health:

Maintaining cognitive health involves a holistic approach that includes:

- **Nutrition:** Consuming a balanced diet rich in antioxidants, healthy fats, vitamins, and minerals to support brain function.

- **Physical Activity:** Regular exercise increases blood flow to the brain and promotes the growth of new neural connections.

- **Mental Stimulation:** Engaging in mentally challenging activities like puzzles, reading, and learning new skills to keep the brain active.

- **Social Interaction:** Maintaining strong social ties and participating in community activities to promote cognitive engagement and emotional well-being.

- **Stress Management:** Practicing mindfulness, meditation, and relaxation techniques to reduce stress and its negative impact on the brain.

The Importance of Brain Fitness

Brain fitness is crucial for maintaining cognitive function and mental sharpness throughout life. Just as physical fitness involves regular exercise to keep the body in good shape, brain fitness requires consistent mental activity to keep the mind agile and healthy. Brain fitness encompasses activities and lifestyle choices that challenge the brain, promote neuroplasticity, and support overall cognitive health.

1. What is Brain Fitness?

Brain fitness refers to the ability of the brain to function efficiently and effectively in daily life. It involves maintaining cognitive abilities such as memory, reasoning, attention, and problem-solving. Brain fitness can be improved through regular mental exercises, a healthy diet, physical activity, social engagement, and adequate sleep.

2. Benefits of Brain Fitness:

- **Enhanced Cognitive Function:** Regular mental stimulation strengthens neural connections, enhances memory, and improves problem-solving skills. Engaging in activities that challenge the brain can delay the onset of cognitive decline.

- **Increased Neuroplasticity:** Brain fitness promotes neuroplasticity, the brain's ability to reorganize itself by forming new neural connections. This adaptability allows the brain to compensate for injury or disease and adjust to new situations or changes in the environment.

- **Better Emotional Regulation:** A fit brain is better equipped to manage stress, anxiety, and depression. It supports emotional regulation, resilience, and mental well-being, leading to improved overall quality of life.

- **Reduced Risk of Cognitive Decline:** Engaging in regular brain fitness activities can help protect against age-related cognitive decline, including conditions such as mild cognitive impairment (MCI) and dementia. Studies have shown that people who maintain an active and engaged mind are less likely to develop Alzheimer's disease and other forms of dementia.

- **Improved Quality of Life:** Maintaining brain fitness enhances the ability to perform everyday tasks, maintain independence, and engage in meaningful activities. It supports social interactions, creativity, and continued learning, contributing to a fulfilling and vibrant life.

3. Key Components of Brain Fitness:

- **Mental Stimulation:** Activities that challenge the brain, such as puzzles, learning new skills, playing musical instruments, or engaging in strategic games, help keep the brain active and improve cognitive function.

- **Physical Exercise:** Physical activity increases blood flow to the brain, promotes the growth of new neurons, and releases chemicals that support brain health. Regular aerobic exercise, such as walking, swimming, or cycling, is particularly beneficial for cognitive function.

- **Nutrition:** A brain-healthy diet that includes antioxidants, omega-3 fatty acids, vitamins, and minerals supports cognitive health. Foods like leafy greens, berries, nuts, and fish are known to boost brain function.

- **Social Engagement:** Social activities that involve communication, collaboration, and emotional connection stimulate cognitive function and help prevent cognitive decline. Staying socially active through community groups, clubs, or regular interaction with friends and family is crucial for brain fitness.

- **Sleep and Relaxation:** Adequate sleep and stress management are essential for cognitive health. Sleep plays a critical role in memory consolidation and brain repair, while relaxation techniques like meditation and mindfulness reduce stress and its negative impact on the brain.

4. How Brain Fitness Works:

- **Strengthening Neural Connections:** Engaging in brain fitness activities reinforces existing neural connections and promotes the formation of new ones. This process helps maintain cognitive abilities and improve overall brain function.

- **Promoting Neurogenesis:** Brain fitness activities, particularly aerobic exercise and learning, promote neurogenesis—the growth of new neurons in the hippocampus, a brain area crucial for memory and learning.

- **Enhancing Cognitive Reserve:** Brain fitness helps build cognitive reserve, the brain's ability to improvise and find alternative ways of functioning in the face of damage. A higher cognitive reserve is associated with a lower risk of cognitive decline and dementia.

5. **Practical Tips for Enhancing Brain Fitness:**

- **Stay Curious and Keep Learning:** Engage in lifelong learning by taking up new hobbies, reading, or attending educational courses.

- **Challenge Your Brain Daily:** Incorporate brain-challenging activities into your routine, such as crossword puzzles, Sudoku, or learning a new language.

- **Maintain a Balanced Diet:** Eat a diet rich in brain-boosting foods, such as vegetables, fruits, whole grains, lean proteins, and healthy fats.

- **Exercise Regularly:** Aim for at least 30 minutes of moderate exercise most days of the week to support both physical and cognitive health.

- **Stay Connected:** Foster relationships and participate in social activities to keep your brain engaged and reduce the risk of cognitive decline.

- **Manage Stress and Sleep Well:** Practice relaxation techniques, such as meditation or yoga, and ensure you get 7-9 hours of quality sleep each night.

Debunking Myths About Dementia and Cognitive Decline

Dementia and cognitive decline are often misunderstood, leading to myths that can cause fear, misinformation, and potentially harmful behaviors. Understanding the truth about cognitive decline and dementia is essential for promoting brain health and encouraging proactive measures to maintain cognitive function. This section will address and debunk some of the most common myths.

1. Myth: Cognitive Decline is an Inevitable Part of Aging

- **Fact:** While it is true that certain cognitive changes, such as slower processing speed or occasional forgetfulness, may occur with age, significant cognitive decline is not inevitable. Many people maintain sharp cognitive function well into their later years. Factors like genetics, lifestyle choices, and overall health play a significant role in determining cognitive health. Engaging in brain-healthy activities, such as regular exercise, mental stimulation, a nutritious diet, and social engagement, can help maintain cognitive function and reduce the risk of decline.

2. Myth: Dementia is Just Memory Loss

- **Fact:** Dementia is not just about memory loss; it is a broad term that describes a range of symptoms affecting memory, thinking, communication, and the ability to perform everyday activities. While memory loss is a common symptom, dementia also impacts other cognitive functions such as language, problem-solving, judgment, and attention. Different types of dementia, such as Alzheimer's disease, vascular dementia, and Lewy body dementia, have unique symptoms and progression patterns.

3. Myth: There is Nothing You Can Do to Prevent Dementia

- **Fact:** There are several evidence-based strategies to reduce the risk of developing dementia or delay its onset. These include maintaining a healthy diet, engaging in regular physical activity, staying mentally and socially active, managing stress, and controlling cardiovascular risk factors like hypertension, diabetes, and cholesterol. Research shows that making positive lifestyle changes can have a significant impact on brain health and may help prevent or delay the onset of cognitive decline and dementia.

4. Myth: Only Older People Get Dementia

- **Fact:** While dementia is more common in older adults, it is not exclusively a disease of the elderly. Early-onset dementia can occur in individuals younger than 65, and while it is less common, it does happen. Factors such as genetics, traumatic brain injuries, and certain health conditions can contribute to earlier onset. However, age remains the most significant risk factor, with the prevalence of dementia increasing with advancing age.

5. Myth: Dementia and Alzheimer's Disease are the Same Thing

- **Fact:** Dementia is an umbrella term that describes a collection of symptoms related to cognitive impairment severe enough to interfere with daily life. Alzheimer's disease is the most common cause of dementia, accounting for 60-80% of cases. However, there are other types of dementia, such as vascular dementia, frontotemporal dementia, and Lewy body dementia, each with different causes, symptoms, and progression patterns. Understanding the difference is important for proper diagnosis, treatment, and care.

6. Myth: You Can Tell if Someone has Dementia by their Behavior

- **Fact:** While certain behaviors, such as confusion, disorientation, or memory problems, may suggest cognitive impairment, these symptoms do not always indicate dementia. Several other conditions, including depression, anxiety, medication side effects, thyroid problems, and vitamin deficiencies, can mimic dementia symptoms. A comprehensive medical evaluation, including cognitive testing and imaging, is essential to accurately diagnose dementia and differentiate it from other conditions.

7. Myth: Supplements and "Brain Boosters" Can Cure or Prevent Dementia

- **Fact:** While some supplements and products are marketed as "brain boosters" or cures for dementia, there is currently no scientific evidence supporting their effectiveness in preventing or curing dementia. The best way to support brain health and reduce the risk of cognitive decline is through a healthy lifestyle, including a balanced diet, regular exercise, mental stimulation, and social engagement. It is always best to consult a healthcare professional before taking any supplements or making significant changes to your diet.

8. Myth: All Memory Loss is a Sign of Dementia

- **Fact:** Not all memory loss is indicative of dementia. Memory lapses, such as forgetting names or misplacing items, can be normal, especially with aging or periods of stress. However, when memory problems become frequent, persistent, and interfere with daily life, it may be a sign of a more serious condition. Mild Cognitive Impairment (MCI) is a condition that involves more memory problems than normal aging but does not yet significantly impact daily activities. Some individuals with MCI may develop dementia over time, but not all do.

9. Myth: Dementia is Caused by a Single Factor

- **Fact:** Dementia is a complex condition influenced by multiple factors, including genetics, lifestyle, and environmental factors. While certain genetic mutations are associated with higher risks of specific types of dementia, such as Alzheimer's disease, most cases result from a combination of genetic, lifestyle, and environmental factors. Understanding this complexity helps in adopting a comprehensive approach to prevention, focusing on controllable risk factors like diet, exercise, mental stimulation, and social engagement.

10. Myth: People with Dementia Cannot Live Meaningful Lives

- **Fact:** People with dementia can still lead meaningful and fulfilling lives, especially when they receive the right support and care. Early diagnosis, appropriate interventions, and support from family, friends, and healthcare professionals can improve the quality of life for individuals with dementia. Engaging in enjoyable activities, maintaining social connections, and creating a supportive environment are vital for enhancing well-being and maintaining dignity and independence.

Chapter 1: Understanding the Brain

Basic Brain Anatomy and Function

Understanding basic brain anatomy and function is crucial for grasping how cognitive processes work and how various brain regions contribute to our daily lives. This section provides an overview of the brain's key structures, their functions, and their roles in maintaining cognitive health.

1. Major Brain Structures

- **Cerebrum**
    - **Overview:** The largest and most visible part of the brain, divided into two hemispheres (left and right), each controlling the opposite side of the body.
    - **Function:** Responsible for higher cognitive functions such as thought, reasoning, planning, and voluntary movement. The cerebrum is divided into four lobes, each with specific roles:
        - **Frontal Lobe:**
            - **Location:** Front part of the brain.
            - **Function:** Involved in executive functions (e.g.,

decision-making, problem-solving), motor control, and emotional regulation.

- **Parietal Lobe:**
    - **Location:** Top and rear part of the brain.
    - **Function:** Processes sensory information from the body (e.g., touch, temperature, pain) and plays a role in spatial orientation and body awareness.
- **Temporal Lobe:**
    - **Location:** Sides of the brain, above the ears.
    - **Function:** Handles auditory processing, language comprehension, and memory formation. Contains the hippocampus, critical for forming new memories.
- **Occipital Lobe:**
    - **Location:** Back of the brain.
    - **Function:** Responsible for visual processing, including interpreting visual

information and recognizing objects and faces.

- **Cerebellum**
  - **Overview:** Located at the back of the brain, beneath the cerebrum.
  - **Function:** Coordinates voluntary movements, balance, and posture. It ensures smooth and precise motor control and contributes to cognitive functions like attention and language.

- **Brainstem**
  - **Overview:** Connects the brain to the spinal cord and comprises the midbrain, pons, and medulla oblongata.
  - **Function:** Controls vital life functions such as breathing, heart rate, and blood pressure. It also regulates sleep-wake cycles and relays signals between the brain and the rest of the body.

- **Limbic System**
  - **Overview:** A set of interconnected structures located deep within the brain.
  - **Key Structures and Functions:**
    - **Hippocampus:** Essential for the formation and retrieval of long-term memories and spatial navigation.

- **Amygdala:** Involved in processing emotions, such as fear and pleasure, and emotional memory.
- **Hypothalamus:** Regulates autonomic functions (e.g., hunger, thirst, temperature regulation) and links the nervous system to the endocrine system through the pituitary gland.

2. Brain Function and Communication

- **Neurons and Synapses**
  - **Neurons:** The fundamental units of the brain, responsible for transmitting information through electrical impulses. Each neuron has a cell body (soma), dendrites (which receive signals), and an axon (which sends signals).
  - **Synapses:** The junctions between neurons where communication occurs. Neurotransmitters are released from one neuron and bind to receptors on the next, facilitating the transmission of signals.

- **Neurotransmitters**
  - **Dopamine:** Associated with reward, motivation, and motor control. Imbalances are linked to conditions such as Parkinson's disease and schizophrenia.

- **Serotonin:** Regulates mood, sleep, and appetite. Low levels are associated with depression and anxiety disorders.
- **Acetylcholine:** Crucial for memory and learning, and involved in muscle activation. Deficits are seen in Alzheimer's disease.
- **GABA (Gamma-Aminobutyric Acid):** An inhibitory neurotransmitter that helps control anxiety and stress responses.
- **Glutamate:** An excitatory neurotransmitter important for learning and memory. Excessive glutamate activity can lead to neurodegenerative conditions.

3. Functional Areas of the Brain

- **Motor Cortex:** Located in the frontal lobe, this area is responsible for voluntary movement control. Different regions of the motor cortex correspond to specific body parts, with greater areas dedicated to more finely controlled movements (e.g., hands and face).
- **Somatosensory Cortex:** Located in the parietal lobe, it processes sensory information from the body, such as touch and temperature. The somatosensory cortex maps sensory inputs from various body parts, similar to the motor cortex.
- **Broca's Area:** Found in the frontal lobe, it is involved in speech production and language

processing. Damage to this area can result in difficulties with speech and language expression.

- **Wernicke's Area:** Located in the temporal lobe, it is crucial for language comprehension. Damage to this area can lead to difficulties understanding language and producing coherent speech.

- **Visual Cortex:** Located in the occipital lobe, it processes visual information from the eyes. It is responsible for interpreting visual stimuli, such as shapes, colors, and movement.

4. Brain Health and Function

Maintaining brain health involves supporting the functions of these key structures and areas through healthy lifestyle choices:

- **Regular Physical Exercise:** Enhances blood flow to the brain and supports neurogenesis, contributing to overall cognitive function and mood regulation.

- **Balanced Nutrition:** Provides essential nutrients that support brain health, such as omega-3 fatty acids, antioxidants, and vitamins.

- **Mental Stimulation:** Engaging in intellectually stimulating activities helps strengthen neural connections and supports cognitive function.

- **Adequate Sleep:** Essential for memory consolidation, cognitive performance, and overall brain health.

- **Social Interaction:** Encourages cognitive engagement and emotional well-being, which are critical for maintaining cognitive health.

How the Brain Ages

As we age, our brains undergo a series of natural changes that affect cognitive function and overall brain health. Understanding these changes is crucial for recognizing what is a normal part of aging versus what might indicate a more serious issue, such as neurodegenerative disease. This section explores the key aspects of brain aging, including structural, functional, and cognitive changes.

1. Structural Changes

- **Brain Volume Reduction:**
    - **Overview:** One of the most noticeable changes with aging is a decrease in brain volume. This reduction is primarily due to the loss of neurons and the shrinkage of certain brain regions.
    - **Affected Areas:** The most significant volume loss occurs in the frontal lobes, which are involved in executive functions, and the hippocampus, which is critical for memory formation.
    - **Impact:** Reduced brain volume can affect cognitive abilities, such as memory and processing speed, but it is not necessarily indicative of a disease.

- **White Matter Changes:**
  - **Overview:** White matter consists of myelinated nerve fibers that connect different brain regions. With age, white matter can degrade, leading to reduced efficiency in communication between brain areas.
  - **Impact:** White matter changes can affect cognitive functions like attention, processing speed, and memory. They are often seen in neuroimaging studies as areas of decreased signal intensity.
- **Neuronal Loss:**
  - **Overview:** While the loss of neurons is part of normal aging, the extent can vary among individuals. Some regions of the brain, such as the prefrontal cortex and hippocampus, are more susceptible to neuronal loss.
  - **Impact:** Neuronal loss can contribute to cognitive decline, but the brain's ability to adapt and compensate (neuroplasticity) often mitigates these effects.

2. Functional Changes

- **Slower Cognitive Processing:**
  - **Overview:** Aging often results in slower cognitive processing speeds. This can affect tasks that require quick thinking or decision-making.

- o **Impact:** While processing speed may decline, other cognitive abilities, such as accumulated knowledge and vocabulary, tend to remain stable or even improve with age.

- **Decline in Working Memory:**
  - o **Overview:** Working memory, which involves holding and manipulating information temporarily, often declines with age. This can affect the ability to multitask and remember information in the short term.
  - o **Impact:** Declines in working memory can impact daily functioning but are usually not severe. Strategies such as using external memory aids or breaking tasks into smaller steps can help manage these challenges.

- **Changes in Executive Function:**
  - o **Overview:** Executive functions, including planning, problem-solving, and decision-making, can become less efficient with age. The frontal lobes, responsible for these functions, are particularly affected.
  - o **Impact:** Difficulties with executive functions can affect complex tasks that require organization and strategic thinking.

3. Cognitive Changes

- **Memory Changes:**
  - **Overview:** Memory changes are a common aspect of aging. While episodic memory (the ability to recall specific events) may decline, semantic memory (knowledge of facts and concepts) often remains stable or improves.
  - **Impact:** Age-related memory changes can result in occasional forgetfulness, but significant memory loss may indicate more serious conditions, such as dementia.
- **Attention and Concentration:**
  - **Overview:** Older adults may experience challenges with sustained attention and concentration. This can affect the ability to focus on tasks for extended periods.
  - **Impact:** Attention-related changes can impact daily activities but can be managed with strategies such as reducing distractions and breaking tasks into smaller segments.
- **Language and Communication:**
  - **Overview:** Language abilities generally remain intact with age, though some older adults may experience mild difficulties with word-finding or recalling names.
  - **Impact:** These changes are usually minor and do not significantly impair

communication. Engaging in conversations and reading can help maintain language skills.

4. Factors Influencing Brain Aging

- **Genetics:**
    - **Overview:** Genetic factors play a role in how the brain ages. Certain genetic variants can influence susceptibility to age-related cognitive decline and neurodegenerative diseases.
    - **Impact:** While genetics is a factor, lifestyle and environmental influences also play a significant role in brain aging.

- **Lifestyle Factors:**
    - **Overview:** Lifestyle choices, such as physical activity, diet, and mental stimulation, have a significant impact on brain health. Healthy habits can mitigate some effects of aging and support cognitive function.
    - **Impact:** Regular exercise, a balanced diet, and engaging in cognitive and social activities can promote brain health and slow the aging process.

- **Health Conditions:**
    - **Overview:** Chronic health conditions, such as cardiovascular disease, diabetes,

and high blood pressure, can impact brain health and accelerate cognitive decline.
- **Impact:** Managing these health conditions through medical care and lifestyle changes can help protect cognitive function.

5. Coping with Age-Related Changes

- **Cognitive Training:**
    - **Overview:** Cognitive training exercises, such as puzzles, memory games, and learning new skills, can help maintain cognitive abilities and promote brain plasticity.
    - **Impact:** Regular cognitive training can enhance mental agility and support cognitive health.
- **Physical Activity:**
    - **Overview:** Physical exercise benefits brain health by increasing blood flow, reducing inflammation, and promoting neurogenesis.
    - **Impact:** Engaging in regular physical activity can improve cognitive function and overall well-being.
- **Healthy Lifestyle Choices:**
    - **Overview:** A balanced diet rich in antioxidants, omega-3 fatty acids, and other nutrients supports brain health.

Adequate sleep and stress management are also crucial.

- **Impact:** Adopting a healthy lifestyle can help maintain cognitive function and improve quality of life as we age.

What Causes Cognitive Decline?

Cognitive decline can result from a variety of factors, ranging from natural aging processes to specific neurological conditions. Understanding these causes helps in identifying preventive measures and managing cognitive health effectively. This section explores the primary contributors to cognitive decline, including physiological changes, diseases, and lifestyle factors.

1. Age-Related Changes

- **Natural Aging:**
    - **Overview:** As people age, normal changes occur in the brain that can affect cognitive function. These changes include reductions in brain volume, neuronal loss, and decreased synaptic density.
    - **Impact:** Age-related cognitive decline often involves slower processing speeds, mild memory issues, and reduced executive function. However, these changes are usually gradual and less severe than those seen in neurodegenerative diseases.

2. Neurodegenerative Diseases

- **Alzheimer's Disease:**
    - **Overview:** Alzheimer's disease is the most common form of dementia, characterized by progressive memory loss, confusion, and difficulty performing daily tasks.
    - **Pathology:** It involves the accumulation of amyloid plaques and tau tangles in the brain, leading to neuronal death and brain shrinkage.
    - **Impact:** Symptoms typically start with mild memory loss and can progress to severe cognitive impairment and loss of independence.

- **Vascular Dementia:**
    - **Overview:** Vascular dementia results from reduced blood flow to the brain due to stroke or other blood vessel issues.
    - **Pathology:** It is characterized by damage to brain regions that control memory and cognitive function due to small strokes or blockages.
    - **Impact:** Symptoms can vary depending on the location and extent of brain damage but often include memory problems, difficulty with planning, and impaired judgment.

- **Lewy Body Dementia:**
    - **Overview:** Lewy body dementia is a type of progressive dementia associated with abnormal protein deposits called Lewy bodies.
    - **Pathology:** It affects areas of the brain that control movement, cognition, and behavior. It often presents with fluctuating cognition, visual hallucinations, and motor symptoms similar to Parkinson's disease.
    - **Impact:** Cognitive fluctuations, hallucinations, and movement difficulties are common symptoms.
- **Frontotemporal Dementia:**
    - **Overview:** Frontotemporal dementia (FTD) primarily affects the frontal and temporal lobes of the brain, leading to changes in behavior, personality, and language.
    - **Pathology:** FTD involves the degeneration of neurons in these specific brain regions, which can result in drastic changes in behavior and social conduct.
    - **Impact:** Symptoms include inappropriate social behavior, difficulty with speech, and a decline in executive function.

3. Cognitive Impairments Due to Medical Conditions

- **Stroke:**
    - **Overview:** A stroke can lead to sudden cognitive impairment due to interruption of blood flow to the brain.
    - **Impact:** Cognitive effects depend on the stroke's location and severity. Common outcomes include problems with memory, attention, and executive function.
- **Traumatic Brain Injury (TBI):**
    - **Overview:** TBI results from head injuries and can cause cognitive impairments that vary from mild to severe.
    - **Impact:** Depending on the injury's extent, symptoms can include memory problems, difficulties with concentration, and changes in mood or behavior.
- **Chronic Illnesses:**
    - **Overview:** Conditions like diabetes, hypertension, and heart disease can negatively impact brain health.
    - **Impact:** Poorly managed chronic illnesses can lead to vascular damage and increased risk of cognitive decline and dementia.

4. Lifestyle Factors

- **Physical Inactivity:**

- **Overview:** Lack of physical exercise can contribute to cognitive decline by reducing blood flow to the brain and promoting the risk of vascular issues.
- **Impact:** Regular physical activity is associated with better cognitive function and reduced risk of dementia.

- **Poor Diet:**
    - **Overview:** Diets high in saturated fats, sugars, and processed foods can negatively impact brain health.
    - **Impact:** Nutrient deficiencies and high levels of inflammation associated with poor diet choices can accelerate cognitive decline.

- **Chronic Stress:**
    - **Overview:** Persistent stress and anxiety can have detrimental effects on brain function.
    - **Impact:** Chronic stress can lead to elevated levels of cortisol, which is associated with hippocampal damage and memory impairment.

- **Sleep Disorders:**
    - **Overview:** Poor sleep quality and sleep disorders, such as sleep apnea, can negatively affect cognitive health.

- **Impact:** Sleep disruptions can impair memory, attention, and executive function, and contribute to the development of dementia.

5. Genetic Factors

- **Genetic Predisposition:**
  - **Overview:** Certain genetic factors can increase the risk of developing cognitive disorders.
  - **Impact:** For example, the presence of the APOE ε4 allele is associated with an increased risk of Alzheimer's disease. However, genetics alone do not determine cognitive health; lifestyle and environmental factors also play a significant role.

6. Environmental and Social Factors

- **Social Isolation:**
  - **Overview:** Limited social interaction can contribute to cognitive decline and accelerate dementia progression.
  - **Impact:** Social engagement is crucial for maintaining cognitive function and emotional well-being.

- **Educational Attainment:**
  - **Overview:** Higher levels of education are associated with better cognitive health and a reduced risk of dementia.

- **Impact:** Educational experiences contribute to cognitive reserve, which helps protect against age-related cognitive decline.

Chapter 2: The Science of Neuroplasticity

What is Neuroplasticity?

Neuroplasticity, also known as brain plasticity, is the brain's remarkable ability to reorganize itself by forming new neural connections throughout life. This capacity for change enables the brain to adapt to new experiences, learn new skills, and recover from injuries. Understanding neuroplasticity is crucial for recognizing how the brain functions and how it can be influenced to support cognitive health and recovery.

1. Definition and Overview

- **Neuroplasticity Defined:**
    - Neuroplasticity refers to the brain's ability to reorganize its structure and function in response to experience, learning, or injury. This plasticity involves changes at various levels, including the molecular, cellular, and network levels.
    - It encompasses both the formation of new synaptic connections and the modification of existing ones, reflecting the brain's dynamic and adaptable nature.
- **Types of Neuroplasticity:**

- **Structural Plasticity:** Refers to physical changes in the brain's structure. This includes the growth of new neurons (neurogenesis) and the strengthening or weakening of synaptic connections.
- **Functional Plasticity:** Involves the brain's ability to shift functions from damaged areas to intact areas. This type of plasticity helps compensate for lost functions due to injury or disease.

2. Historical Perspective

- **Early Understanding:**
  - Historically, the brain was believed to be relatively static after development, with limited capacity for change. It was thought that once mature, the brain's structure and function were largely fixed.

- **Modern Advances:**
  - Research over the past few decades has demonstrated that the brain remains plastic throughout life. Studies using brain imaging, animal models, and clinical observations have revealed that the brain can adapt to new experiences, learn new skills, and recover from injuries through neuroplastic processes.

3. Mechanisms of Neuroplasticity

- **Synaptic Plasticity:**

- **Overview:** Changes in the strength and efficiency of synaptic connections between neurons.
- **Key Mechanisms:**
  - **Long-Term Potentiation (LTP):** The process by which synaptic connections are strengthened based on recent activity. LTP is essential for learning and memory formation.
  - **Long-Term Depression (LTD):** The process by which synaptic connections are weakened. LTD helps in eliminating unnecessary information and fine-tuning neural circuits.

- **Neurogenesis:**
  - **Overview:** The formation of new neurons from neural stem cells. Neurogenesis primarily occurs in the hippocampus, a region involved in learning and memory.
  - **Influencing Factors:** Factors such as physical exercise, environmental enrichment, and certain types of learning can promote neurogenesis.
- **Functional Reorganization:**
  - **Overview:** The brain's ability to reassign functions from damaged areas to healthy areas. This is particularly important for

recovery following brain injuries or strokes.

- **Examples:** After a stroke, functions that were previously performed by damaged brain regions can be taken over by adjacent or contralateral brain areas.

4. Types of Neuroplasticity

- **Experience-Dependent Plasticity:**
  - **Overview:** Changes in the brain's structure and function based on individual experiences and learning.
  - **Examples:** Learning a new skill, practicing a musical instrument, or engaging in novel experiences can lead to structural and functional changes in the brain.

- **Developmental Plasticity:**
  - **Overview:** The changes in the brain that occur as a result of development from infancy through adulthood.
  - **Examples:** Critical periods during development when the brain is highly plastic and sensitive to environmental influences, such as language acquisition and sensory development.

- **Reactive Plasticity:**
  - **Overview:** The brain's ability to adapt in response to injury or damage.

- **Examples:** Recovery of function after brain injury or stroke through reorganization of neural networks and recruitment of alternative brain areas.

5. Importance of Neuroplasticity

- **Learning and Memory:**
  - **Overview:** Neuroplasticity underpins the brain's ability to learn new information, acquire new skills, and form memories. It supports cognitive development and adaptation throughout life.

- **Recovery from Injury:**
  - **Overview:** Neuroplasticity is crucial for recovery following brain injuries or strokes. It allows for the reorganization of neural networks and the restoration of lost functions.

- **Adaptation to Change:**
  - **Overview:** The brain's adaptability enables individuals to cope with new experiences, changes in the environment, and evolving cognitive demands.

6. Promoting Neuroplasticity

- **Engaging in New Experiences:**
  - **Overview:** Actively engaging in new and challenging activities stimulates neuroplasticity.

- **Examples:** Learning new skills, taking up hobbies, and participating in complex cognitive tasks.

- **Maintaining a Healthy Lifestyle:**
    - **Overview:** Physical exercise, a balanced diet, adequate sleep, and stress management all support brain health and neuroplasticity.
    - **Impact:** These factors contribute to optimal brain function and promote structural and functional changes.

- **Mental Stimulation:**
    - **Overview:** Cognitive activities such as puzzles, games, and learning new information support neuroplasticity.
    - **Impact:** Regular mental stimulation enhances cognitive abilities and supports overall brain health.

How Neuroplasticity Can Reverse Damage

Neuroplasticity plays a crucial role in the brain's ability to recover from damage and adapt to new conditions. This capacity for change allows the brain to reorganize itself, compensate for lost functions, and repair damage through various mechanisms. This section explores how neuroplasticity contributes to reversing damage and enhancing recovery.

1. **Understanding Brain Damage and Its Impact**
   - **Types of Brain Damage:**
     - **Stroke:** Interruption of blood flow to the brain, leading to neuronal death and functional loss.
     - **Traumatic Brain Injury (TBI):** Physical injury to the brain causing damage to neurons and brain structures.
     - **Neurodegenerative Diseases:** Conditions such as Alzheimer's disease and Parkinson's disease that progressively damage brain cells.
   - **Impact of Brain Damage:**
     - Damage can result in cognitive, motor, and sensory impairments, affecting various aspects of daily life, including memory, movement, and perception.

2. **Mechanisms of Neuroplasticity in Reversing Damage**
   - **Functional Reorganization:**
     - **Overview:** The brain's ability to reorganize functions from damaged areas to intact regions.
     - **Mechanism:** When a specific brain area is damaged, other regions may take over the lost functions through adaptive reorganization.

- - **Example:** After a stroke affecting speech areas, adjacent or contralateral brain regions may compensate for the loss, helping to restore language abilities.

- **Synaptic Plasticity:**
  - **Overview:** Changes in the strength and efficiency of synaptic connections can help the brain adapt and recover from damage.
  - **Mechanism:** Strengthening existing synapses or forming new connections can enhance neural communication and compensate for lost functions.
  - **Example:** In rehabilitation, targeted exercises can promote synaptic plasticity, aiding recovery of motor functions.

- **Neurogenesis:**
  - **Overview:** The formation of new neurons, primarily in the hippocampus, which supports cognitive functions and recovery.
  - **Mechanism:** Neurogenesis helps replace lost neurons and supports brain plasticity by integrating new neurons into existing neural networks.
  - **Example:** Environmental enrichment and physical exercise can stimulate neurogenesis and support recovery following brain injury.

3. Rehabilitation Techniques to Enhance Neuroplasticity

- **Cognitive Rehabilitation:**
    - **Overview:** Therapies designed to improve cognitive functions affected by brain damage.
    - **Techniques:** Include cognitive exercises, memory training, and problem-solving tasks that stimulate neural activity and promote plasticity.
    - **Impact:** These therapies help individuals regain cognitive functions and adapt to new ways of performing tasks.

- **Physical Rehabilitation:**
    - **Overview:** Interventions focused on restoring motor functions and physical abilities.
    - **Techniques:** Include physical therapy, occupational therapy, and motor training exercises that encourage brain reorganization and motor recovery.
    - **Impact:** Regular practice of physical tasks can enhance motor skills and support recovery of movement abilities.

- **Speech and Language Therapy:**
    - **Overview:** Therapies aimed at improving communication skills affected by brain damage.

- o **Techniques:** Include exercises to enhance speech production, language comprehension, and communication strategies.
- o **Impact:** Speech and language therapy can help individuals regain or improve their ability to communicate effectively.

4. Enhancing Neuroplasticity for Recovery

- **Engaging in Rehabilitation Exercises:**
  - o **Overview:** Structured and repetitive exercises tailored to stimulate neuroplasticity and support recovery.
  - o **Examples:** Practice tasks that target specific impairments, such as hand movements for motor recovery or cognitive drills for memory enhancement.
- **Maintaining a Healthy Lifestyle:**
  - o **Overview:** Physical exercise, a balanced diet, adequate sleep, and stress management contribute to brain health and recovery.
  - o **Impact:** A healthy lifestyle supports neuroplasticity and enhances the effectiveness of rehabilitation efforts.
- **Participating in Cognitive and Social Activities:**

- **Overview:** Engaging in stimulating cognitive and social activities can support brain function and recovery.
- **Examples:** Social interactions, mental challenges, and learning new skills can enhance neuroplasticity and contribute to overall recovery.

5. Case Studies and Research Findings

- **Case Study Examples:**
    - **Stroke Rehabilitation:** Studies have shown that individuals who engage in intensive rehabilitation therapy exhibit significant recovery due to neuroplastic changes in the brain.
    - **Traumatic Brain Injury (TBI) Recovery:** Research demonstrates that targeted rehabilitation and cognitive exercises can lead to substantial improvements in function and quality of life.
- **Research Insights:**
    - **Neuroplasticity Research:** Ongoing research continues to uncover how neuroplasticity can be harnessed to support recovery from brain damage and improve treatment outcomes.

Practical Applications of Neuroplasticity in Daily Life

Understanding neuroplasticity can empower individuals to actively support their cognitive health and overall well-being through daily activities and lifestyle choices. This section explores practical ways to apply the principles of neuroplasticity in everyday life to enhance brain function, promote learning, and support recovery.

1. Cognitive Stimulation

- **Engaging in Lifelong Learning:**
    - **Overview:** Continuously challenging the brain with new and complex tasks promotes neuroplasticity.
    - **Examples:** Learning a new language, playing a musical instrument, or acquiring new skills can stimulate brain activity and encourage the formation of new neural connections.

- **Mental Exercises:**
    - **Overview:** Activities that challenge cognitive functions help strengthen and maintain brain networks.
    - **Examples:** Puzzles, brain games, and strategy-based activities such as chess or Sudoku can enhance memory, problem-solving skills, and cognitive flexibility.

- **Reading and Creative Thinking:**
  - **Overview:** Engaging in reading and creative activities stimulates brain regions involved in language, imagination, and critical thinking.
  - **Examples:** Reading books, writing, drawing, or engaging in artistic pursuits can support cognitive health and creativity.

2. Physical Exercise

- **Regular Physical Activity:**
  - **Overview:** Exercise promotes neuroplasticity by increasing blood flow to the brain, reducing inflammation, and stimulating neurogenesis.
  - **Examples:** Activities such as walking, jogging, swimming, or strength training can support brain health and improve cognitive function.
- **Incorporating Variety:**
  - **Overview:** A diverse exercise routine engages different brain regions and supports overall brain health.
  - **Examples:** Combining aerobic exercises with strength training, coordination exercises, and balance training can provide comprehensive benefits.

3. Healthy Lifestyle Choices

- **Balanced Diet:**
  - **Overview:** Nutrient-rich foods support brain function and neuroplasticity.
  - **Examples:** Consuming foods high in omega-3 fatty acids, antioxidants, vitamins, and minerals can enhance cognitive health. Examples include fish, nuts, berries, and leafy greens.
- **Adequate Sleep:**
  - **Overview:** Quality sleep is essential for cognitive function and memory consolidation.
  - **Recommendations:** Aim for 7-9 hours of sleep per night, maintain a consistent sleep schedule, and create a restful sleep environment.
- **Stress Management:**
  - **Overview:** Chronic stress can impair neuroplasticity and cognitive function.
  - **Techniques:** Practice relaxation techniques such as mindfulness, meditation, deep breathing, or yoga to manage stress and support brain health.

4. Social Interaction

- **Maintaining Social Connections:**
  - **Overview:** Engaging in social activities and maintaining relationships supports

cognitive function and emotional well-being.

- **Examples:** Participate in social gatherings, volunteer work, or community events to stimulate brain activity and foster emotional support.

- **Meaningful Conversations:**

  - **Overview:** Engaging in discussions and meaningful conversations challenges cognitive processes and promotes mental stimulation.

  - **Examples:** Regularly conversing with friends, family, or colleagues can enhance language skills and cognitive engagement.

5. Cognitive and Physical Rehabilitation

- **Personalized Rehabilitation Programs:**

  - **Overview:** Tailored rehabilitation programs can support recovery from brain injury or cognitive impairments by leveraging neuroplasticity.

  - **Examples:** Work with healthcare professionals to design individualized rehabilitation programs that include cognitive exercises, physical therapy, and occupational therapy.

- **Setting Goals and Tracking Progress:**

  - **Overview:** Setting specific goals and monitoring progress can enhance

motivation and support neuroplasticity during rehabilitation.
- o **Examples:** Use tools such as progress trackers or journals to set achievable goals and celebrate milestones in cognitive and physical recovery.

6. Creating a Stimulating Environment

- **Environmental Enrichment:**
  - o **Overview:** An enriched environment that offers cognitive, sensory, and social stimulation can promote neuroplasticity.
  - o **Examples:** Surround yourself with stimulating activities, engaging experiences, and opportunities for learning and creativity.
- **Designing a Brain-Friendly Space:**
  - o **Overview:** Create a living or work environment that supports cognitive health and reduces stress.
  - o **Examples:** Organize your space to be conducive to productivity, relaxation, and mental stimulation.

7. Integrating Neuroplasticity Practices into Daily Routine

- **Routine and Habit Formation:**

- **Overview:** Incorporate neuroplasticity-promoting activities into your daily routine to create lasting benefits.
- **Examples:** Establish regular schedules for physical exercise, cognitive stimulation, and social interactions to reinforce healthy habits and support brain function.

- **Balancing Activities:**
  - **Overview:** Balance various activities to ensure comprehensive support for neuroplasticity and overall well-being.
  - **Examples:** Combine cognitive, physical, and social activities in your daily life to promote holistic brain health.

Chapter 3: Nutrition for Brain Health

Essential Nutrients for Cognitive Function

Cognitive function relies on a variety of nutrients that support brain health, neurotransmitter production, and overall mental performance. This section explores the essential nutrients that play a vital role in maintaining and enhancing cognitive function.

1. Omega-3 Fatty Acids

- **Importance for Cognitive Function:**
    - **Brain Structure:** Omega-3 fatty acids, particularly DHA (docosahexaenoic acid), are crucial for the structural integrity of brain cell membranes.
    - **Neurotransmission:** Support the fluidity of neuronal membranes, which is essential for effective neurotransmission and synaptic plasticity.
    - **Anti-Inflammatory Effects:** Help reduce inflammation in the brain, which is linked to cognitive decline.
- **Sources:**
    - Fatty fish (salmon, mackerel, sardines)

- Flaxseeds and flaxseed oil
- Chia seeds
- Walnuts
- Algae-based supplements (for a vegetarian/vegan option)

2. Antioxidants

- **Importance for Cognitive Function:**
    - **Oxidative Stress Protection:** Antioxidants protect brain cells from oxidative damage caused by free radicals.
    - **Cognitive Health:** Help reduce the risk of neurodegenerative diseases and support cognitive function.
- **Key Antioxidants:**
    - **Vitamin C:** Essential for protecting brain cells and supporting neurotransmitter function.
    - **Vitamin E:** Provides neuroprotective effects by reducing oxidative stress.
    - **Flavonoids and Polyphenols:** Found in fruits and vegetables, these compounds have anti-inflammatory and antioxidant properties.
- **Sources:**
    - Vitamin C: Citrus fruits (oranges, strawberries), bell peppers, broccoli

- Vitamin E: Nuts (almonds, hazelnuts), seeds, spinach
- Flavonoids/Polyphenols: Berries (blueberries, strawberries), dark chocolate, green tea

3. B Vitamins

- **Importance for Cognitive Function:**
    - **Energy Production:** B vitamins are involved in energy metabolism, which is critical for brain function.
    - **Neurotransmitter Synthesis:** Essential for the production of neurotransmitters like serotonin and dopamine.
    - **Cognitive Health:** B vitamins support overall brain health and may help prevent cognitive decline.

- **Key B Vitamins:**
    - **B1 (Thiamine):** Supports cognitive function and energy production.
    - **B6 (Pyridoxine):** Involved in neurotransmitter synthesis and cognitive processes.
    - **B9 (Folate):** Essential for brain development and function, and helps reduce homocysteine levels.
    - **B12 (Cobalamin):** Supports myelin sheath formation and cognitive function.

- **Sources:**
    - B1: Whole grains, legumes, nuts, seeds
    - B6: Poultry, fish, bananas, chickpeas
    - B9: Leafy greens, legumes, fortified grains
    - B12: Animal products (meat, dairy, eggs), fortified plant-based milks

4. Vitamin D

- **Importance for Cognitive Function:**
    - **Neuronal Health:** Supports brain cell growth and function, and modulates neurotransmitter systems.
    - **Mood Regulation:** Influences mood and cognitive health, with deficiencies linked to cognitive impairments.
- **Sources:**
    - Sunlight exposure (the skin produces vitamin D when exposed to sunlight)
    - Fatty fish (salmon, mackerel)
    - Fortified foods (milk, orange juice, cereals)
    - Vitamin D supplements (especially in areas with limited sunlight)

5. Minerals

- **Iron:**

- o **Importance for Cognitive Function:** Crucial for oxygen transport and energy production in the brain.
- o **Sources:** Red meat, poultry, lentils, spinach, fortified cereals

- **Magnesium:**
  - o **Importance for Cognitive Function:** Supports neurotransmitter function, brain plasticity, and stress management.
  - o **Sources:** Nuts (almonds, cashews), seeds, leafy greens, whole grains

- **Zinc:**
  - o **Importance for Cognitive Function:** Involved in neurotransmission, synaptic plasticity, and brain signaling.
  - o **Sources:** Shellfish, meat, legumes, seeds, nuts

6. Amino Acids

- **Importance for Cognitive Function:**
  - o **Neurotransmitter Production:** Amino acids are the building blocks of neurotransmitters, which are essential for brain communication and cognitive processes.
- **Key Amino Acids:**

- - **Tyrosine:** Precursor to dopamine and norepinephrine, which influence mood and cognitive function.
  - **Tryptophan:** Precursor to serotonin, affecting mood and cognitive function.
  - **Glutamine:** Important for cognitive function and brain metabolism.
- **Sources:**
  - Tyrosine: Lean meats, dairy products, soy products, eggs
  - Tryptophan: Turkey, dairy products, nuts, seeds
  - Glutamine: Meat, dairy, eggs, beans

7. Practical Tips for Incorporating These Nutrients

- **Balanced Diet:**
  - **Overview:** Aim for a varied diet that includes a wide range of nutrient-dense foods to ensure adequate intake of essential nutrients.
  - **Tips:** Incorporate fatty fish, leafy greens, nuts, seeds, and a variety of fruits and vegetables into daily meals.
- **Meal Planning:**
  - **Overview:** Plan meals to include foods rich in essential nutrients.

- **Tips:** Create balanced meal plans that combine sources of omega-3s, antioxidants, B vitamins, and other key nutrients.

- **Mindful Eating:**
  - **Overview:** Focus on whole foods and minimize processed food intake to support brain health.
  - **Tips:** Opt for fresh, whole ingredients and prepare meals at home to maintain control over nutrient intake.

The Impact of Diet on Brain Health

Diet significantly influences brain health, cognitive function, and the risk of neurological disorders. This section explores how various dietary patterns, foods, and nutrients impact brain health and cognitive performance.

1. How Diet Affects Cognitive Function

- **Nutrient Supply:**
  - **Overview:** The brain requires a steady supply of nutrients to function optimally. A diet rich in essential nutrients supports cognitive processes such as memory, learning, and decision-making.
  - **Impact:** Deficiencies in key nutrients can impair brain function and increase the risk of cognitive decline.

- **Neurotransmitter Production:**
    - **Overview:** Nutrients from the diet are crucial for the production of neurotransmitters, which are chemicals that transmit signals in the brain.
    - **Impact:** Adequate levels of neurotransmitters support mood regulation, focus, and overall cognitive performance.
- **Inflammation and Oxidative Stress:**
    - **Overview:** Chronic inflammation and oxidative stress are linked to cognitive decline and neurodegenerative diseases.
    - **Impact:** Diets high in antioxidants and anti-inflammatory foods can reduce oxidative damage and support brain health.

2. Dietary Patterns and Their Effects

- **Mediterranean Diet:**
    - **Overview:** Emphasizes whole grains, fruits, vegetables, nuts, seeds, fish, and olive oil while limiting red meat and processed foods.
    - **Impact:** Associated with lower risk of cognitive decline and neurodegenerative diseases. Supports brain health through antioxidants, healthy fats, and anti-inflammatory compounds.

- **DASH Diet:**
    - **Overview:** Focuses on reducing sodium intake and increasing consumption of fruits, vegetables, whole grains, and lean proteins.
    - **Impact:** Supports cardiovascular health, which is closely linked to brain health. Helps reduce blood pressure and inflammation, contributing to cognitive well-being.
- **Plant-Based Diets:**
    - **Overview:** Emphasizes plant-based foods such as fruits, vegetables, legumes, nuts, and seeds while minimizing animal products.
    - **Impact:** Rich in antioxidants, healthy fats, and fiber, supporting cognitive function and reducing the risk of cognitive decline.
- **Western Diet:**
    - **Overview:** Characterized by high intake of processed foods, sugary snacks, and unhealthy fats.
    - **Impact:** Associated with increased risk of cognitive decline, inflammation, and neurodegenerative diseases. High sugar and fat content can impair brain function and increase oxidative stress.

3. The Role of Specific Foods in Brain Health

- **Fatty Fish:**
    - **Overview:** Rich in omega-3 fatty acids, particularly DHA, which supports brain cell structure and function.
    - **Impact:** Enhances cognitive performance, reduces inflammation, and supports overall brain health.
- **Berries:**
    - **Overview:** High in antioxidants, particularly flavonoids, which protect brain cells from oxidative damage.
    - **Impact:** Improves memory and cognitive function, and reduces the risk of neurodegenerative diseases.
- **Leafy Greens:**
    - **Overview:** Rich in vitamins (e.g., vitamin K) and minerals (e.g., folate) that support brain health.
    - **Impact:** Enhances cognitive function and reduces the risk of cognitive decline.
- **Nuts and Seeds:**
    - **Overview:** Provide healthy fats, antioxidants, and essential nutrients such as vitamin E and magnesium.
    - **Impact:** Support cognitive health, reduce inflammation, and improve brain function.

- **Whole Grains:**
    - **Overview:** Source of complex carbohydrates, fiber, and B vitamins.
    - **Impact:** Provides sustained energy for brain function and supports overall cognitive health.
- **Turmeric:**
    - **Overview:** Contains curcumin, which has anti-inflammatory and antioxidant properties.
    - **Impact:** May enhance cognitive function and reduce the risk of neurodegenerative diseases.

4. The Impact of Diet on Neurological Disorders

- **Alzheimer's Disease:**
    - **Overview:** Diets high in antioxidants, omega-3 fatty acids, and anti-inflammatory foods may reduce the risk of Alzheimer's disease.
    - **Impact:** Certain dietary patterns, like the Mediterranean diet, are associated with lower risk and slower progression of the disease.
- **Parkinson's Disease:**
    - **Overview:** Nutrient-rich diets that support brain health may help manage symptoms and improve quality of life.

- - **Impact:** Anti-inflammatory and antioxidant-rich foods can support overall brain function and reduce disease-related inflammation.
- **Depression and Anxiety:**
  - **Overview:** Nutrients such as omega-3 fatty acids, B vitamins, and antioxidants play a role in mood regulation.
  - **Impact:** A balanced diet can support mental health and potentially alleviate symptoms of depression and anxiety.

5. Practical Tips for a Brain-Healthy Diet

- **Incorporate a Variety of Nutrient-Dense Foods:**
  - **Overview:** Aim for a balanced diet that includes a wide range of nutrient-rich foods to support brain health.
  - **Tips:** Include a variety of fruits, vegetables, whole grains, lean proteins, and healthy fats in your meals.
- **Reduce Intake of Processed Foods:**
  - **Overview:** Minimize consumption of processed and sugary foods that can negatively impact brain health.
  - **Tips:** Opt for whole, unprocessed foods and limit intake of foods high in added sugars and unhealthy fats.

- **Stay Hydrated:**
    - **Overview:** Adequate hydration is essential for cognitive function and overall brain health.
    - **Tips:** Drink plenty of water throughout the day and include hydrating foods such as fruits and vegetables in your diet.
- **Plan Balanced Meals:**
    - **Overview:** Create meals that incorporate a balance of macronutrients and essential nutrients.
    - **Tips:** Include sources of healthy fats, lean proteins, and complex carbohydrates in each meal to support brain function.

Brain-Boosting Foods and Recipes

Incorporating brain-boosting foods into your diet can enhance cognitive function, improve memory, and support overall brain health. This section highlights key brain-boosting foods and provides practical recipes to include these nutritious ingredients in your meals.

1. Key Brain-Boosting Foods

- **Fatty Fish:**
    - **Benefits:** Rich in omega-3 fatty acids (especially DHA), which support brain cell structure, reduce inflammation, and enhance cognitive function.

- ○ **Examples:** Salmon, mackerel, sardines.
- **Berries:**
  - ○ **Benefits:** High in antioxidants and flavonoids that protect the brain from oxidative stress and improve memory.
  - ○ **Examples:** Blueberries, strawberries, raspberries.
- **Leafy Greens:**
  - ○ **Benefits:** Provide essential vitamins (e.g., vitamin K, folate) and antioxidants that support brain health and cognitive function.
  - ○ **Examples:** Spinach, kale, Swiss chard.
- **Nuts and Seeds:**
  - ○ **Benefits:** Offer healthy fats, vitamin E, and antioxidants that support brain health and reduce inflammation.
  - ○ **Examples:** Walnuts, almonds, chia seeds, flaxseeds.
- **Whole Grains:**
  - ○ **Benefits:** Source of complex carbohydrates and B vitamins that provide sustained energy and support cognitive function.
  - ○ **Examples:** Oats, quinoa, brown rice.
- **Avocados:**

- **Benefits:** Rich in healthy fats, antioxidants, and vitamins that promote brain health and improve blood flow.
- **Examples:** Avocado slices, avocado spread.

- **Turmeric:**
  - **Benefits:** Contains curcumin, which has anti-inflammatory and antioxidant properties that may enhance cognitive function and protect against neurodegenerative diseases.
  - **Examples:** Turmeric root, turmeric powder.

- **Dark Chocolate:**
  - **Benefits:** Contains flavonoids, caffeine, and antioxidants that improve cognitive function and mood.
  - **Examples:** 70% or higher cocoa content dark chocolate.

- **Eggs:**
  - **Benefits:** Provide choline, which is crucial for neurotransmitter production and cognitive function.
  - **Examples:** Scrambled eggs, omelets.

2. Brain-Boosting Recipes

Recipe 1: Omega-3 Rich Salmon Salad

- **Ingredients:**
  - 1 salmon fillet
  - 4 cups mixed leafy greens (spinach, kale, arugula)
  - 1/2 avocado, sliced
  - 1/4 cup walnuts, chopped
  - 1/2 cup blueberries
  - 2 tbsp olive oil
  - 1 tbsp lemon juice
  - Salt and pepper to taste
- **Instructions:**

1. Season the salmon fillet with salt and pepper. Grill or bake until cooked through (about 5-7 minutes per side).

2. In a large bowl, combine leafy greens, avocado slices, walnuts, and blueberries.

3. Flake the cooked salmon and add it to the salad.

4. Drizzle with olive oil and lemon juice. Toss gently to combine.

Recipe 2: Berry and Chia Seed Smoothie

- **Ingredients:**
  - 1 cup almond milk (or other plant-based milk)

- 1/2 cup mixed berries (blueberries, strawberries)
- 1 tbsp chia seeds
- 1 tbsp honey or maple syrup (optional)
- 1/2 banana (optional for added creaminess)

- **Instructions:**

1. Combine all ingredients in a blender.
2. Blend until smooth and creamy.
3. Pour into a glass and enjoy immediately.

Recipe 3: Spinach and Mushroom Quinoa Bowl

- **Ingredients:**
  - 1 cup quinoa
  - 2 cups water or vegetable broth
  - 1 cup fresh spinach
  - 1/2 cup mushrooms, sliced
  - 1 tbsp olive oil
  - 1 garlic clove, minced
  - 1 tbsp soy sauce or tamari
  - Salt and pepper to taste

- **Instructions:**

1. Rinse the quinoa under cold water. Combine with water or broth in a pot and bring to a boil. Reduce

heat and simmer for 15 minutes, or until the quinoa is cooked and water is absorbed.

2. In a skillet, heat olive oil over medium heat. Add garlic and cook until fragrant.

3. Add mushrooms and cook until tender. Add spinach and cook until wilted.

4. Stir in cooked quinoa and soy sauce. Season with salt and pepper to taste.

Recipe 4: Turmeric and Coconut Energy Balls

- **Ingredients:**
    - 1 cup almonds
    - 1 cup medjool dates, pitted
    - 1/4 cup shredded coconut
    - 1 tbsp turmeric powder
    - 1 tbsp coconut oil
- **Instructions:**

1. Place almonds in a food processor and pulse until finely chopped.

2. Add dates, shredded coconut, turmeric powder, and coconut oil. Process until the mixture sticks together.

3. Roll the mixture into small balls and refrigerate for at least 1 hour before serving.

Recipe 5: Dark Chocolate and Nut Bark

- **Ingredients:**
  - 1 cup dark chocolate chips (70% cocoa or higher)
  - 1/4 cup mixed nuts (almonds, walnuts, pistachios), roughly chopped
  - Sea salt (optional)
- **Instructions:**

1. Melt the dark chocolate chips in a microwave-safe bowl or using a double boiler, stirring until smooth.

2. Pour the melted chocolate onto a parchment-lined baking sheet and spread evenly.

3. Sprinkle the chopped nuts over the chocolate and press gently.

4. Chill in the refrigerator until the chocolate is set. Break into pieces and enjoy.

3. Tips for Incorporating Brain-Boosting Foods

- **Meal Planning:** Plan meals around brain-boosting ingredients to ensure a balanced intake of nutrients.
- **Snack Wisely:** Keep brain-boosting snacks like nuts, berries, and dark chocolate on hand for a quick and healthy boost.
- **Experiment with Recipes:** Try new recipes that incorporate a variety of brain-boosting foods to keep meals interesting and nutritious.

- **Stay Consistent:** Regularly include brain-boosting foods in your diet to support long-term cognitive health.

Chapter 4: Exercise and the Brain

Physical Exercise and Cognitive Health

Physical exercise has profound effects on cognitive health and function. This section delves into how various forms of exercise influence cognitive processes, the underlying mechanisms at play, and practical strategies to maximize cognitive benefits through physical activity.

1. Mechanisms Linking Exercise to Cognitive Health

- **Increased Blood Flow to the Brain:**
    - **Overview:** Exercise boosts cerebral blood flow, delivering more oxygen and nutrients to brain cells.
    - **Impact:** Improved blood flow supports cognitive functions such as memory, learning, and overall brain health.
- **Neurogenesis and Synaptic Plasticity:**
    - **Overview:** Exercise stimulates the growth of new neurons and strengthens synaptic connections in the brain.

- **Impact:** Enhances learning and memory capabilities and supports recovery from brain injuries.

- **Brain-Derived Neurotrophic Factor (BDNF):**
  - **Overview:** Physical activity increases BDNF levels, a protein that promotes neuron survival, growth, and synaptic plasticity.
  - **Impact:** Supports cognitive function and may protect against neurodegenerative diseases.

- **Reduction of Inflammation and Oxidative Stress:**
  - **Overview:** Exercise reduces systemic inflammation and oxidative stress, which are linked to cognitive decline.
  - **Impact:** Helps protect the brain from damage and supports overall cognitive health.

- **Regulation of Neurotransmitters:**
  - **Overview:** Exercise influences neurotransmitter levels, including serotonin, dopamine, and norepinephrine.
  - **Impact:** Affects mood, cognition, and emotional regulation.

2. Cognitive Benefits of Different Types of Exercise

- **Aerobic Exercise:**
  - **Overview:** Activities that increase heart rate and breathing, such as running, swimming, or cycling.
  - **Benefits:** Improves executive function, memory, and overall cognitive performance. Regular aerobic exercise is associated with a lower risk of cognitive decline and dementia.
- **Strength Training:**
  - **Overview:** Exercises that build muscle strength, including weight lifting and resistance training.
  - **Benefits:** Enhances cognitive function, particularly in areas related to memory and executive function. Strength training also contributes to overall brain health and physical fitness.
- **Balance and Coordination Exercises:**
  - **Overview:** Activities that improve balance and coordination, such as tai chi and yoga.
  - **Benefits:** Enhances spatial awareness, motor control, and cognitive function. These exercises are particularly beneficial for older adults to prevent falls and maintain cognitive function.
- **Mind-Body Exercises:**

- - **Overview:** Exercises that combine physical movement with mental focus, such as meditation and qigong.
  - **Benefits:** Reduces stress, improves emotional regulation, and supports cognitive function through relaxation techniques.

3. Impact of Exercise on Specific Cognitive Functions

- **Memory:**
  - **Overview:** Aerobic exercise and strength training improve memory function by increasing BDNF and supporting neurogenesis.
  - **Strategies:** Incorporate regular aerobic activities and strength training to enhance memory retention and recall.

- **Attention and Focus:**
  - **Overview:** Exercise improves attention and focus by enhancing brain connectivity and function.
  - **Strategies:** Engage in physical activities that require coordination and concentration to boost attention.

- **Executive Function:**
  - **Overview:** Regular exercise supports executive functions such as planning, problem-solving, and decision-making.

- **Strategies:** Incorporate varied and challenging workouts to stimulate cognitive processes related to executive function.

- **Mood and Emotional Well-Being:**
  - **Overview:** Exercise helps regulate mood by increasing levels of neurotransmitters and reducing symptoms of anxiety and depression.
  - **Strategies:** Regular physical activity can improve mood and support overall mental health.

4. Practical Recommendations for Maximizing Cognitive Benefits

- **Consistency is Key:**
  - **Overview:** Regular exercise is essential for maintaining cognitive health and reaping long-term benefits.
  - **Recommendations:** Aim for at least 150 minutes of moderate-intensity aerobic exercise or 75 minutes of vigorous activity per week, combined with muscle-strengthening activities.

- **Variety in Exercise Routine:**
  - **Overview:** A diverse exercise routine provides a range of cognitive and physical benefits.

- **Recommendations:** Include a mix of aerobic, strength, balance, and mind-body exercises to support overall brain health.

- **Incorporate Cognitive Challenges:**
  - **Overview:** Exercise that includes cognitive challenges, such as learning new movements or complex coordination, can enhance cognitive benefits.
  - **Recommendations:** Try new exercise classes, sports, or activities that challenge both body and mind.

- **Set Realistic Goals:**
  - **Overview:** Setting achievable fitness goals helps maintain motivation and adherence to an exercise routine.
  - **Recommendations:** Start with manageable goals and gradually increase intensity and duration.

- **Monitor Progress and Adapt:**
  - **Overview:** Tracking progress helps assess the impact of exercise on cognitive health and allows for adjustments.
  - **Recommendations:** Use a journal or fitness app to monitor workouts and cognitive improvements.

5. Overcoming Barriers to Exercise

- **Time Constraints:**

- o **Strategies:** Break workouts into shorter sessions, incorporate physical activity into daily routines, and prioritize exercise in your schedule.

- **Motivation Issues:**
  - o **Strategies:** Find enjoyable activities, set specific goals, and consider working out with a partner or group for accountability.

- **Physical Limitations:**
  - o **Strategies:** Choose low-impact exercises, such as swimming or walking, and consult with a healthcare provider for personalized recommendations.

- **Environmental Constraints:**
  - o **Strategies:** Create a home exercise space, use online workout programs, and find local fitness opportunities.

Types of Exercises That Improve Brain Function

Exercise is a powerful tool for enhancing cognitive function and overall brain health. Different types of exercises offer unique benefits, and incorporating a variety of activities can maximize cognitive improvements. This section explores the various types of exercises that support brain function and their specific benefits.

1. **Aerobic Exercise**

    - **Overview:**
        - **Definition:** Activities that increase heart rate and breathing, improving cardiovascular fitness.
        - **Examples:** Running, swimming, cycling, brisk walking.
    - **Benefits:**
        - **Cognitive Enhancement:** Improves memory, attention, and executive function by increasing cerebral blood flow and stimulating neurogenesis.
        - **Mental Health:** Reduces symptoms of anxiety and depression through the release of endorphins and improved regulation of stress hormones.
    - **Recommended Activities:**
        - **Running or Jogging:** Improves cardiovascular health and supports cognitive function.
        - **Swimming:** Combines full-body exercise with low-impact benefits, ideal for all fitness levels.
        - **Cycling:** Enhances endurance and stimulates brain function through rhythmic movement.

2. **Strength Training**

- **Overview:**
  - **Definition:** Exercises that build muscle strength through resistance.
  - **Examples:** Weight lifting, resistance band exercises, bodyweight exercises like squats and lunges.
- **Benefits:**
  - **Cognitive Improvement:** Supports memory and executive function by promoting the release of growth factors and enhancing neuroplasticity.
  - **Physical Health:** Improves muscle mass, bone density, and metabolic health.
- **Recommended Activities:**
  - **Free Weights:** Develop strength and coordination while supporting cognitive function.
  - **Resistance Bands:** Provide a versatile, low-impact option for strength training.
  - **Bodyweight Exercises:** Use exercises like push-ups, planks, and squats to build strength and cognitive resilience.

3. Balance and Coordination Exercises

- **Overview:**

- - **Definition:** Activities that enhance balance, coordination, and spatial awareness.
  - **Examples:** Yoga, tai chi, balance drills, and stability exercises.
- **Benefits:**
  - **Cognitive Function:** Improves spatial awareness, motor control, and executive function.
  - **Fall Prevention:** Reduces the risk of falls, particularly in older adults, by improving balance and coordination.
- **Recommended Activities:**
  - **Yoga:** Combines physical movement with mental focus to enhance balance, flexibility, and cognitive function.
  - **Tai Chi:** Integrates slow, deliberate movements with deep breathing to improve balance and mental clarity.
  - **Balance Drills:** Use exercises like single-leg stands and balance board training to enhance stability.

4. Mind-Body Exercises

- **Overview:**
  - **Definition:** Exercises that combine physical movement with mental focus and relaxation techniques.

- **Examples:** Meditation, qigong, and mindful walking.

- **Benefits:**
  - **Stress Reduction:** Lowers cortisol levels and reduces anxiety, supporting overall cognitive function.
  - **Mental Clarity:** Enhances focus, emotional regulation, and cognitive performance through relaxation techniques.

- **Recommended Activities:**
  - **Meditation:** Practice mindfulness or guided meditation to reduce stress and improve mental clarity.
  - **Qigong:** Engage in gentle, flowing movements combined with deep breathing to promote relaxation and cognitive health.
  - **Mindful Walking:** Combine walking with mindfulness techniques to enhance cognitive function and mental well-being.

5. High-Intensity Interval Training (HIIT)

- **Overview:**
  - **Definition:** Alternating between short bursts of intense exercise and periods of rest or low-intensity activity.

- - **Examples:** Sprint intervals, circuit training, and Tabata workouts.
- **Benefits:**
  - **Cognitive Function:** Enhances executive function, memory, and attention by promoting neurogenesis and improving brain plasticity.
  - **Physical Health:** Boosts cardiovascular fitness, metabolic rate, and muscle strength.
- **Recommended Activities:**
  - **Sprint Intervals:** Alternate between short, intense sprints and recovery periods to improve brain function and physical fitness.
  - **Circuit Training:** Combine different exercises, such as jumping jacks, burpees, and squats, for a comprehensive workout.
  - **Tabata Workouts:** Perform 20 seconds of high-intensity exercise followed by 10 seconds of rest for a quick and effective workout.

6. Social and Recreational Activities

- **Overview:**
  - **Definition:** Exercises that involve social interaction and recreation.

- **Examples:** Dancing, team sports, and group fitness classes.
- **Benefits:**
    - **Cognitive Function:** Enhances mood, social engagement, and cognitive stimulation through interactive activities.
    - **Social Interaction:** Provides opportunities for social connection, which can support mental health and cognitive function.
- **Recommended Activities:**
    - **Dancing:** Engage in various styles of dance to improve coordination, memory, and social interaction.
    - **Team Sports:** Participate in sports like soccer, basketball, or volleyball to enhance cognitive function and social well-being.
    - **Group Fitness Classes:** Join classes like aerobics or spin to combine exercise with social interaction.

7. Functional Training

- **Overview:**
    - **Definition:** Exercises that mimic everyday movements to improve overall functionality and mobility.

- - **Examples:** Functional movement patterns, such as squatting, lunging, and lifting.
- **Benefits:**
  - **Cognitive Function:** Enhances coordination and motor skills, supporting cognitive processes related to movement and balance.
  - **Physical Health:** Improves strength, flexibility, and functional capacity for daily activities.
- **Recommended Activities:**
  - **Functional Movement Patterns:** Practice exercises that mimic daily activities, such as carrying groceries or climbing stairs.
  - **Mobility Drills:** Incorporate exercises that improve joint range of motion and overall functional capacity.

Creating a Brain-Healthy Fitness Routine

Establishing a fitness routine that promotes brain health involves integrating a variety of exercises that support cognitive function, emotional well-being, and overall physical fitness. This section provides practical steps for designing a balanced fitness regimen that maximizes cognitive benefits and supports long-term brain health.

1. Assess Your Current Fitness Level

- **Evaluate Physical Fitness:**
    - **Overview:** Assess your current level of fitness to determine appropriate exercise intensity and types.
    - **Methods:** Perform basic fitness tests, such as a walking or running test, strength assessments, and flexibility evaluations.
- **Identify Cognitive Goals:**
    - **Overview:** Define your cognitive goals, such as improving memory, attention, or executive function.
    - **Methods:** Consider your cognitive strengths and areas for improvement, and set specific, measurable objectives.

2. Set Realistic Goals

- **Short-Term Goals:**
    - **Overview:** Establish achievable goals to build momentum and track progress.
    - **Examples:** Commit to exercising 3 times a week for 30 minutes, or incorporate 10 minutes of daily mindfulness meditation.
- **Long-Term Goals:**

- **Overview:** Set broader goals for sustained brain health and overall fitness.
- **Examples:** Aim for 150 minutes of aerobic exercise per week, or participate in a new fitness class within the next 3 months.

- **SMART Goals:**
  - **Overview:** Use the SMART criteria (Specific, Measurable, Achievable, Relevant, Time-bound) to set clear and actionable goals.
  - **Examples:** "I will run for 20 minutes, 3 times a week, for the next 6 weeks to improve my cardiovascular health and cognitive function."

3. Design a Balanced Exercise Program

- **Include Aerobic Exercise:**
  - **Overview:** Incorporate activities that increase heart rate and improve cardiovascular health.
  - **Recommendations:** Aim for at least 150 minutes of moderate-intensity aerobic activity per week.
  - **Examples:** Brisk walking, jogging, cycling, swimming.

- **Add Strength Training:**

- o **Overview:** Include exercises that build muscle strength and support cognitive function.
- o **Recommendations:** Perform strength training exercises on 2 or more days per week.
- o **Examples:** Weight lifting, bodyweight exercises, resistance band workouts.

- **Incorporate Balance and Coordination Exercises:**
  - o **Overview:** Engage in activities that enhance balance, coordination, and spatial awareness.
  - o **Recommendations:** Include balance and coordination exercises 2-3 times per week.
  - o **Examples:** Yoga, tai chi, balance board exercises.

- **Integrate Mind-Body Exercises:**
  - o **Overview:** Practice exercises that combine physical movement with mental focus and relaxation.
  - o **Recommendations:** Incorporate mind-body exercises 1-2 times per week.
  - o **Examples:** Meditation, qigong, mindful walking.

- **Include Flexibility and Mobility Work:**

- **Overview:** Perform exercises that improve joint flexibility and range of motion.
- **Recommendations:** Stretch regularly and incorporate flexibility exercises into your routine.
- **Examples:** Static stretching, dynamic stretching, mobility drills.

4. Create a Weekly Workout Schedule

- **Example Weekly Schedule:**
  - **Monday:** 30 minutes of aerobic exercise (e.g., jogging) + 10 minutes of stretching.
  - **Tuesday:** 30 minutes of strength training (e.g., weight lifting) + 10 minutes of balance exercises.
  - **Wednesday:** 30 minutes of mind-body exercise (e.g., yoga or meditation).
  - **Thursday:** 30 minutes of aerobic exercise (e.g., cycling) + 10 minutes of mobility drills.
  - **Friday:** 30 minutes of strength training (e.g., bodyweight exercises) + 10 minutes of flexibility exercises.
  - **Saturday:** 30 minutes of recreational activity (e.g., dancing, hiking) + 10 minutes of stretching.

- **Sunday:** Rest day or gentle activity (e.g., mindful walking).

- **Adjusting the Schedule:**
    - **Overview:** Modify the schedule based on personal preferences, fitness level, and goals.
    - **Tips:** Adapt the duration, intensity, and types of exercises as needed.

5. Incorporate Cognitive Challenges

- **Engage in Learning Activities:**
    - **Overview:** Combine physical exercise with cognitive challenges to enhance brain function.
    - **Examples:** Learn new dance routines, try different sports, or participate in cognitive training games.

- **Variety in Exercise:**
    - **Overview:** Incorporate diverse exercises to stimulate different cognitive functions and prevent monotony.
    - **Examples:** Alternate between aerobic activities, strength training, and mind-body exercises.

- **Social Interaction:**

- **Overview:** Participate in group fitness classes or team sports to combine physical activity with social engagement.
- **Examples:** Join a fitness class, play team sports, or exercise with friends.

6. Monitor Progress and Adjust

- **Track Your Progress:**
  - **Overview:** Use tools to monitor fitness levels, cognitive improvements, and adherence to your routine.
  - **Examples:** Fitness apps, exercise journals, cognitive assessments.

- **Evaluate and Adjust:**
  - **Overview:** Regularly assess your progress and make adjustments to your routine as needed.
  - **Tips:** Review goals, modify exercises, and seek feedback to ensure continued improvement.

7. Stay Motivated

- **Find Enjoyable Activities:**
  - **Overview:** Choose exercises that you enjoy to maintain motivation and adherence.
  - **Examples:** Select activities that match your interests and preferences.

- **Set Rewards:**
    - **Overview:** Reward yourself for achieving fitness milestones and maintaining consistency.
    - **Examples:** Treat yourself to a new workout outfit or a relaxing activity.
- **Stay Accountable:**
    - **Overview:** Use accountability partners or groups to stay motivated and committed.
    - **Examples:** Exercise with a friend, join a fitness community, or work with a personal trainer.

Chapter 5: Mental Exercises and Brain Training

Cognitive Exercises to Enhance Memory and Focus

Memory and focus are critical components of cognitive health. Engaging in specific cognitive exercises can help improve these abilities, enhance overall brain function, and support mental sharpness. This section provides various exercises designed to boost memory and concentration.

1. Memory Enhancement Exercises

- **Memory Recall Techniques:**
    - **Overview:** Exercises that challenge your ability to recall information and strengthen memory retention.
    - **Examples:**
        - **Repetition:** Repeat information or lists several times to reinforce memory. For example, memorize a phone number or a list of items by repeating them aloud or writing them down.
        - **Visualization:** Create mental images of information to enhance recall. For instance, visualize a

grocery list as a story or a series of pictures in your mind.

- **Mnemonics and Memory Aids:**
    - **Overview:** Use mnemonic devices to improve memory and recall.
    - **Examples:**
        - **Acronyms:** Create acronyms to remember lists or sequences. For example, use the acronym "HOMES" to remember the Great Lakes (Huron, Ontario, Michigan, Erie, Superior).
        - **Rhymes and Songs:** Create rhymes or songs to remember information. For example, use a rhyme to memorize a list of historical dates or scientific terms.

- **Chunking:**
    - **Overview:** Break down large pieces of information into smaller, manageable chunks to improve memory retention.
    - **Examples:**
        - **Phone Numbers:** Remember phone numbers by breaking them into smaller groups (e.g., 123-456-7890 instead of 1234567890).
        - **Lists:** Chunk grocery lists into categories (e.g., fruits, vegetables,

dairy) to make them easier to remember.

- **Memory Games and Puzzles:**
    - **Overview:** Engage in games and puzzles designed to challenge and improve memory.
    - **Examples:**
        - **Matching Games:** Play card games where you match pairs of cards to enhance visual memory.
        - **Crossword Puzzles:** Solve crossword puzzles to stimulate memory recall and word knowledge.

2. Focus and Concentration Exercises

- **Attention Training Exercises:**
    - **Overview:** Activities designed to improve attention span and reduce distractibility.
    - **Examples:**
        - **Concentration Drills:** Practice focusing on a single task or object for a set period, gradually increasing the duration. For instance, focus on a candle flame or a simple object for 5 minutes without distractions.

- **Attention Apps:** Use digital tools and apps designed to improve concentration and attention, such as focused work timers or attention training games.

- **Mindfulness and Meditation:**
    - **Overview:** Techniques that enhance focus and concentration by promoting mindfulness and reducing mental clutter.
    - **Examples:**
        - **Mindfulness Meditation:** Practice mindfulness meditation by focusing on your breath and observing thoughts without judgment. Aim for 10-15 minutes daily.
        - **Guided Meditations:** Use guided meditation apps or recordings to help improve focus and concentration through structured meditation sessions.

- **Task Management Techniques:**
    - **Overview:** Strategies to improve focus and productivity by managing tasks effectively.
    - **Examples:**
        - **Pomodoro Technique:** Work in focused intervals (e.g., 25 minutes)

followed by short breaks (e.g., 5 minutes) to maintain concentration and prevent burnout.

- **Task Lists:** Create and prioritize task lists to organize and manage tasks efficiently, enhancing focus and productivity.

- **Mind-Body Coordination Exercises:**
  - **Overview:** Activities that combine physical movement with mental focus to improve concentration and cognitive function.
  - **Examples:**
    - **Yoga:** Engage in yoga poses and practices that require mental focus and physical coordination, enhancing overall concentration.
    - **Tai Chi:** Practice tai chi movements to improve mind-body coordination and mental clarity.

3. Cognitive Stimulation Activities

- **Learning New Skills:**
  - **Overview:** Engage in activities that challenge the brain and promote cognitive growth.
  - **Examples:**

- **Learning a New Language:** Stimulates memory and cognitive processes by challenging the brain with new vocabulary and grammar rules.
- **Playing a Musical Instrument:** Enhances cognitive abilities related to memory, coordination, and auditory processing.

- **Problem-Solving and Strategy Games:**
  - **Overview:** Play games that require strategic thinking and problem-solving skills to stimulate cognitive function.
  - **Examples:**
    - **Chess:** Engage in chess to improve strategic thinking, problem-solving, and memory.
    - **Sudoku:** Solve Sudoku puzzles to challenge logical reasoning and concentration.

- **Mental Flexibility Exercises:**
  - **Overview:** Activities that promote cognitive flexibility and adaptability by challenging the brain to switch between tasks or perspectives.
  - **Examples:**

- **Brain Teasers:** Solve brain teasers and riddles that require creative thinking and mental flexibility.
- **Dual-Tasking:** Practice dual-tasking exercises, such as walking while solving math problems or performing mental calculations.

4. Strategies for Incorporating Cognitive Exercises into Daily Life

- **Routine Integration:**
  - **Overview:** Incorporate cognitive exercises into your daily routine for consistent mental stimulation.
  - **Examples:**
    - **Daily Puzzles:** Solve a crossword puzzle or play a memory game each day as part of your morning routine.
    - **Mindfulness Practice:** Dedicate a few minutes each day to mindfulness meditation or focused breathing exercises.
- **Social Engagement:**
  - **Overview:** Engage in social activities that challenge cognitive skills and promote mental stimulation.
  - **Examples:**

- **Discussion Groups:** Participate in discussion groups or book clubs that encourage critical thinking and cognitive engagement.
- **Social Games:** Play board games or card games with friends and family to stimulate cognitive function and social interaction.

- **Variety and Challenge:**
  - **Overview:** Incorporate a variety of cognitive exercises to keep the brain engaged and challenged.
  - **Examples:**
    - **Exercise Variety:** Alternate between different types of cognitive exercises, such as memory games, puzzles, and problem-solving activities.
    - **Challenge Progression:** Gradually increase the difficulty level of exercises to continue challenging the brain and promoting cognitive growth.

Puzzles, Games, and Activities for Brain Health

Engaging in puzzles, games, and various activities can significantly contribute to brain health by stimulating cognitive functions, enhancing problem-solving skills, and promoting mental agility. This section provides an overview of different types of brain-boosting activities and how they can be incorporated into daily life for optimal cognitive benefits.

1. Types of Puzzles for Brain Health

- **Crossword Puzzles:**
    - **Overview:** Word puzzles that challenge vocabulary, general knowledge, and problem-solving skills.
    - **Benefits:** Enhances verbal memory, improves language skills, and stimulates cognitive functions.
    - **Tips:** Start with easier puzzles and gradually move to more complex ones to keep the challenge engaging.
- **Sudoku:**
    - **Overview:** Number placement puzzles that require logical reasoning and pattern recognition.
    - **Benefits:** Boosts logical thinking, attention to detail, and problem-solving skills.
    - **Tips:** Practice regularly and try different levels of difficulty to improve cognitive flexibility.
- **Jigsaw Puzzles:**

- **Overview:** Picture puzzles that involve assembling pieces to form a complete image.
- **Benefits:** Enhances visual-spatial reasoning, memory, and concentration.
- **Tips:** Choose puzzles with varying piece counts and complexity to challenge different cognitive skills.

- **Logic Puzzles:**
    - **Overview:** Puzzles that require deductive reasoning and critical thinking to solve.
    - **Benefits:** Improves problem-solving abilities, logical reasoning, and mental agility.
    - **Tips:** Engage with different types of logic puzzles, such as riddles, brainteasers, and lateral thinking puzzles.

2. Brain Games for Cognitive Enhancement

- **Memory Games:**
    - **Overview:** Games designed to improve memory and recall abilities.
    - **Examples:**
        - **Matching Games:** Find pairs of cards or images to enhance visual and short-term memory.

- **Sequence Games:** Recall and repeat sequences of numbers, letters, or patterns to boost working memory.

- **Strategy Games:**
  - **Overview:** Games that involve planning, strategizing, and decision-making.
  - **Examples:**
    - **Chess:** Enhances strategic thinking, problem-solving skills, and cognitive flexibility.
    - **Go:** Improves strategic planning, pattern recognition, and mental endurance.

- **Word Games:**
  - **Overview:** Games that focus on vocabulary, word formation, and language skills.
  - **Examples:**
    - **Scrabble:** Boosts vocabulary and cognitive skills by forming words from letter tiles.
    - **Boggle:** Improves word recall and visual recognition by finding words in a grid of letters.

- **Math Games:**

- - **Overview:** Games that challenge numerical reasoning and arithmetic skills.
  - **Examples:**
    - **KenKen:** Enhances mathematical problem-solving abilities by solving numeric puzzles with specific constraints.
    - **Math Bingo:** Reinforces arithmetic skills by solving math problems to achieve bingo.

3. Activities for Cognitive Stimulation

- **Brain Training Apps:**
  - **Overview:** Digital tools designed to provide structured cognitive exercises and track progress.
  - **Examples:**
    - **Lumosity:** Offers a variety of games targeting memory, attention, problem-solving, and more.
    - **Elevate:** Provides exercises focused on language skills, math, and cognitive functions.
- **Creative Activities:**
  - **Overview:** Engaging in creative pursuits that stimulate cognitive processes and enhance brain health.

- Examples:
  - **Drawing or Painting:** Improves visual-spatial skills, creativity, and relaxation.
  - **Writing:** Enhances cognitive function by practicing writing, journaling, or creative storytelling.
- **Learning New Skills:**
  - **Overview:** Acquiring new skills or hobbies that challenge the brain and promote cognitive growth.
  - **Examples:**
    - **Learning a Musical Instrument:** Stimulates auditory processing, coordination, and memory.
    - **Cooking or Baking:** Engages cognitive skills related to planning, following instructions, and sensory experiences.

4. Social Games and Activities

- **Board Games:**
  - **Overview:** Social games that involve strategy, negotiation, and problem-solving.
  - **Examples:**

- **Monopoly:** Enhances strategic thinking, financial management, and social interaction.
- **Catan:** Improves negotiation skills, resource management, and strategic planning.

- **Card Games:**
  - **Overview:** Games that involve strategy, memory, and cognitive skills.
  - **Examples:**
    - **Poker:** Boosts memory, strategic thinking, and decision-making under pressure.
    - **Bridge:** Enhances memory, strategy, and teamwork skills.

- **Group Activities:**
  - **Overview:** Social activities that promote cognitive engagement through interaction and teamwork.
  - **Examples:**
    - **Trivia Games:** Improves general knowledge, memory recall, and social interaction.
    - **Discussion Groups:** Stimulates cognitive function by engaging in conversations and debates on various topics.

5. Incorporating Puzzles and Games into Daily Life

- **Routine Integration:**
    - **Overview:** Incorporate puzzles, games, and activities into your daily routine for consistent cognitive stimulation.
    - **Examples:**
        - **Daily Puzzles:** Solve a crossword puzzle or Sudoku each day as part of your morning routine.
        - **Game Nights:** Schedule regular game nights with friends or family to enjoy social and cognitive benefits.

- **Variety and Challenge:**
    - **Overview:** Engage in a variety of puzzles and games to keep the brain stimulated and challenged.
    - **Examples:**
        - **Rotate Activities:** Alternate between different types of puzzles and games to challenge various cognitive skills.
        - **Increase Difficulty:** Gradually increase the complexity of puzzles and games to continue challenging the brain.

- **Social Engagement:**

- **Overview:** Use social games and group activities to combine cognitive stimulation with social interaction.
- **Examples:**
  - **Participate in Clubs:** Join a trivia club or board game group to engage in cognitive activities and social interaction.
  - **Organize Game Events:** Host game nights or puzzle-solving sessions with friends and family.

The Role of Lifelong Learning in Cognitive Longevity

Lifelong learning is a key component in maintaining cognitive health and longevity. Engaging in continuous learning throughout life has been shown to support brain function, enhance mental agility, and reduce the risk of cognitive decline. This section explores the significance of lifelong learning and provides strategies for integrating learning into everyday life to support cognitive longevity.

1. Understanding Lifelong Learning

- **Definition:**
  - **Overview:** Lifelong learning refers to the ongoing, voluntary, and self-motivated pursuit of knowledge and skills throughout an individual's life.

- **Purpose:** To foster personal development, enhance cognitive abilities, and adapt to changing environments.
- **Benefits:**
  - **Cognitive Health:** Stimulates brain activity, supports neuroplasticity, and reduces the risk of cognitive decline.
  - **Personal Growth:** Enhances self-esteem, adaptability, and overall quality of life.

2. The Impact of Lifelong Learning on Cognitive Longevity

- **Cognitive Stimulation:**
  - **Overview:** Engaging in new learning activities stimulates various cognitive functions and keeps the brain active.
  - **Benefits:** Improves memory, attention, problem-solving skills, and cognitive flexibility.
- **Neuroplasticity:**
  - **Overview:** Lifelong learning supports neuroplasticity, the brain's ability to reorganize and adapt by forming new neural connections.
  - **Benefits:** Enhances the brain's capacity to recover from damage and adapt to new challenges.
- **Reduced Risk of Cognitive Decline:**

- **Overview:** Regular cognitive engagement through learning activities is associated with a lower risk of developing cognitive impairments, such as dementia.
- **Benefits:** Helps maintain cognitive function and delay the onset of age-related cognitive decline.

3. Strategies for Lifelong Learning

- **Formal Education:**
  - **Overview:** Structured learning environments, such as academic courses and professional development programs.
  - **Examples:**
    - **Continuing Education:** Enroll in courses or workshops related to your field or personal interests.
    - **Certifications and Degrees:** Pursue additional qualifications or degrees to enhance knowledge and skills.
- **Self-Directed Learning:**
  - **Overview:** Independent learning activities that individuals pursue on their own.
  - **Examples:**
    - **Online Courses:** Use platforms like Coursera, edX, or Khan

Academy to take courses on various subjects.
- **Books and Journals:** Read books, research papers, and journals to explore new topics and stay informed.

- **Hobbies and Interests:**
  - **Overview:** Engaging in hobbies and activities that challenge the brain and promote learning.
  - **Examples:**
    - **Learning a New Language:** Stimulates cognitive processes and improves memory.
    - **Playing Musical Instruments:** Enhances auditory processing, coordination, and cognitive skills.

- **Social Learning:**
  - **Overview:** Learning through interaction and collaboration with others.
  - **Examples:**
    - **Discussion Groups:** Participate in book clubs, discussion forums, or study groups to share knowledge and engage in intellectual conversations.

- **Workshops and Seminars:** Attend events that provide opportunities for learning and networking.

4. Integrating Lifelong Learning into Daily Life

- **Daily Learning Habits:**
  - **Overview:** Incorporate learning activities into your daily routine to maintain cognitive engagement.
  - **Examples:**
    - **Daily Reading:** Dedicate time each day to read books, articles, or educational material.
    - **Learning Apps:** Use educational apps or platforms to engage in learning activities and track progress.

- **Setting Learning Goals:**
  - **Overview:** Establish personal learning goals to stay motivated and focused on continuous improvement.
  - **Examples:**
    - **Skill Development:** Set goals for acquiring new skills or knowledge in specific areas of interest.
    - **Progress Tracking:** Monitor and evaluate progress towards

learning goals to stay motivated and celebrate achievements.

- **Creating a Learning-Friendly Environment:**
    - **Overview:** Design an environment that supports and encourages ongoing learning.
    - **Examples:**
        - **Learning Space:** Set up a dedicated space for reading, studying, or engaging in educational activities.
        - **Resource Access:** Ensure access to educational resources, such as books, online courses, and learning materials.

5. The Social and Emotional Benefits of Lifelong Learning

- **Social Interaction:**
    - **Overview:** Lifelong learning often involves social activities that provide opportunities for interaction and connection.
    - **Benefits:** Enhances social engagement, reduces feelings of isolation, and fosters a sense of community.
- **Emotional Well-being:**

- o **Overview:** Engaging in learning activities contributes to emotional satisfaction and a sense of accomplishment.
- o **Benefits:** Boosts self-esteem, reduces stress, and promotes overall mental well-being.

6. Overcoming Barriers to Lifelong Learning

- **Time Management:**
  - o **Overview:** Balancing learning with other responsibilities and activities.
  - o **Strategies:** Prioritize learning activities, set aside dedicated time for learning, and incorporate learning into daily routines.

- **Access to Resources:**
  - o **Overview:** Finding and utilizing educational resources and opportunities.
  - o **Strategies:** Explore online platforms, local community programs, and libraries to access learning materials and opportunities.

- **Motivation and Mindset:**
  - o **Overview:** Maintaining motivation and a positive attitude towards learning.
  - o **Strategies:** Set achievable goals, seek support from peers or mentors, and celebrate progress and achievements.

Chapter 6: Stress Management and Brain Health

The Impact of Stress on Cognitive Function

Stress affects various aspects of cognitive function, from memory and attention to problem-solving abilities. Understanding how stress impacts cognitive processes is crucial for developing effective strategies to mitigate its negative effects and maintain optimal brain health. This section delves into the mechanisms by which stress influences cognitive function and the implications for mental performance.

1. The Stress Response

- **Physiological Mechanisms:**
    - **Overview:** Stress triggers the body's "fight-or-flight" response, leading to the release of stress hormones such as cortisol and adrenaline.
    - **Effects:** Acute stress can enhance alertness and focus temporarily, but chronic stress has detrimental effects on cognitive function.
- **Hormonal Influence:**

- o **Cortisol:** Elevated cortisol levels can disrupt brain function, particularly in areas related to memory and emotional regulation.
- o **Adrenaline:** Increased adrenaline can heighten arousal and attention, but prolonged exposure can lead to cognitive impairments.

2. **Impact on Memory**
   - **Short-Term Memory:**
     - o **Overview:** Stress can impair short-term memory, affecting the ability to hold and process information over brief periods.
     - o **Mechanisms:** High cortisol levels can affect the hippocampus, a brain region crucial for short-term memory formation and recall.
   - **Long-Term Memory:**
     - o **Overview:** Chronic stress can also impact long-term memory by affecting the consolidation of new information and retrieval of stored memories.
     - o **Mechanisms:** Persistent stress can lead to structural changes in the hippocampus and impair synaptic plasticity, affecting memory consolidation.
   - **Emotional Memory:**

- **Overview:** Stress can alter the way emotional memories are encoded and recalled.
- **Mechanisms:** Stress can enhance the emotional intensity of memories, making them more vivid but also more prone to distortion.

3. Impact on Attention and Focus

- **Attention Span:**
  - **Overview:** Stress can reduce the ability to maintain focus and sustain attention on tasks.
  - **Mechanisms:** High stress levels can lead to increased distractibility and reduced cognitive control, affecting the ability to concentrate.
- **Selective Attention:**
  - **Overview:** Stress can impair selective attention, making it challenging to filter out irrelevant information and focus on important tasks.
  - **Mechanisms:** Stress can affect the prefrontal cortex, which is responsible for executive functions like selective attention and cognitive control.
- **Cognitive Flexibility:**

- Overview: Stress can limit cognitive flexibility, the ability to switch between tasks or adapt to new information.
- Mechanisms: Chronic stress can impair the brain's ability to adapt to changing situations, affecting problem-solving and decision-making abilities.

4. Impact on Executive Function

- **Planning and Organization:**
  - Overview: Stress can hinder executive functions such as planning, organization, and decision-making.
  - Mechanisms: Prolonged stress can affect the prefrontal cortex, which is responsible for higher-order cognitive processes like goal-setting and task management.

- **Problem-Solving Skills:**
  - Overview: Stress can impair problem-solving abilities, making it more difficult to find solutions to complex issues.
  - Mechanisms: Stress can reduce cognitive resources available for problem-solving and increase reliance on automatic or less effective strategies.

- **Impulsivity and Risk-Taking:**

- **Overview:** Stress can increase impulsivity and risk-taking behavior, affecting decision-making processes.
- **Mechanisms:** Stress can impair the brain's ability to evaluate risks and consequences, leading to more impulsive and less considered decisions.

5. Stress and Cognitive Decline

- **Long-Term Effects:**
  - **Overview:** Chronic stress is associated with an increased risk of cognitive decline and neurodegenerative diseases.
  - **Mechanisms:** Ongoing stress can contribute to inflammation, oxidative stress, and neuronal damage, which are linked to conditions like Alzheimer's disease.

- **Neurodegenerative Diseases:**
  - **Overview:** Prolonged stress can exacerbate the progression of neurodegenerative diseases and accelerate cognitive decline.
  - **Mechanisms:** Stress-related factors such as inflammation and disrupted neurotransmitter systems can contribute to the development and progression of cognitive disorders.

6. Strategies for Mitigating the Impact of Stress on Cognitive Function

- **Stress Management Techniques:**
    - **Overview:** Implementing effective stress management strategies can help protect cognitive function and improve overall brain health.
    - **Techniques:**
        - **Mindfulness and Meditation:** Practice mindfulness and meditation to reduce stress levels and enhance cognitive function.
        - **Physical Exercise:** Engage in regular physical activity to reduce stress and support cognitive health.
        - **Healthy Lifestyle:** Adopt a balanced diet, prioritize sleep, and maintain social connections to mitigate the effects of stress on cognitive function.
- **Cognitive Training and Mental Exercises:**
    - **Overview:** Engage in cognitive training and mental exercises to strengthen cognitive functions and counteract the effects of stress.
    - **Techniques:**

- **Brain Games:** Participate in puzzles, games, and activities that challenge cognitive skills and promote mental agility.
- **Learning New Skills:** Pursue new learning opportunities and hobbies to keep the brain active and engaged.

Mindfulness, Meditation, and Relaxation Techniques

Mindfulness, meditation, and relaxation techniques are powerful tools for managing stress and supporting cognitive health. These practices help cultivate mental clarity, emotional balance, and overall well-being. This section explores the benefits of these techniques and provides practical guidance on how to incorporate them into daily life.

1. Understanding Mindfulness

- **Definition:**
  - **Overview:** Mindfulness is the practice of being fully present and engaged in the current moment, with an attitude of non-judgmental awareness.
  - **Purpose:** To enhance self-awareness, reduce stress, and improve overall mental health.
- **Benefits:**

- - **Cognitive Function:** Improves attention, focus, and memory by training the mind to stay present and resist distractions.
  - **Emotional Regulation:** Helps manage emotions by increasing awareness of emotional states and reducing reactivity.
- **Mindfulness Practices:**
  - **Mindful Breathing:** Focus on the sensation of your breath as you inhale and exhale, bringing attention back to your breath when the mind wanders.
  - **Body Scan:** Conduct a mental scan of your body, paying attention to physical sensations and areas of tension.
  - **Mindful Eating:** Eat slowly and attentively, savoring each bite and noticing the flavors, textures, and sensations of the food.

2. Meditation Techniques

- **Overview:**
  - **Definition:** Meditation involves focusing the mind on a specific object, thought, or activity to achieve mental clarity, relaxation, and self-awareness.
  - **Types:** There are various forms of meditation, each with unique techniques and benefits.
- **Types of Meditation:**

- **Mindfulness Meditation:**
  - **Overview:** Focuses on maintaining awareness of the present moment without judgment.
  - **Practice:** Sit comfortably, close your eyes, and focus on your breath. When your mind wanders, gently bring your attention back to your breath.
- **Loving-Kindness Meditation (Metta):**
  - **Overview:** Cultivates feelings of compassion and love towards oneself and others.
  - **Practice:** Sit comfortably, and silently repeat phrases such as "May I be happy, may I be healthy" while visualizing yourself and others receiving these positive wishes.
- **Transcendental Meditation:**
  - **Overview:** Uses a mantra—a specific word or sound repeated silently—to achieve a state of restful awareness.
  - **Practice:** Sit comfortably, close your eyes, and silently repeat your chosen mantra, allowing it to focus your mind and transcend ordinary thought.

- Guided Meditation:
  - **Overview:** Involves listening to a guide or recording that leads you through a meditation session.
  - **Practice:** Follow the guidance provided, which may include visualization, relaxation techniques, or affirmations.

- **Benefits of Meditation:**
  - **Stress Reduction:** Lowers cortisol levels and promotes relaxation.
  - **Enhanced Focus:** Improves concentration and cognitive function.
  - **Emotional Balance:** Supports emotional regulation and reduces symptoms of anxiety and depression.

3. Relaxation Techniques

- **Overview:**
  - **Definition:** Techniques designed to promote physical and mental relaxation, reducing stress and tension.
  - **Purpose:** To support overall well-being and enhance cognitive function.

- **Techniques:**
  - **Deep Breathing Exercises:**

- **Overview:** Involves taking slow, deep breaths to activate the body's relaxation response.
- **Practice:** Inhale deeply through your nose, hold for a few seconds, and exhale slowly through your mouth. Repeat several times to calm the mind and body.

- Progressive Muscle Relaxation (PMR):
  - **Overview:** Involves tensing and then relaxing different muscle groups to release physical tension.
  - **Practice:** Start with your toes and work your way up through each muscle group, tensing for a few seconds before releasing and relaxing.

- Autogenic Training:
  - **Overview:** Uses self-suggestions and imagery to induce relaxation and promote a sense of calm.
  - **Practice:** Sit or lie down comfortably and use phrases such as "My arms are heavy and warm" to create a sensation of relaxation and comfort.

- Visualization:

- **Overview:** Involves imagining a peaceful or calming scene to promote relaxation and reduce stress.
- **Practice:** Close your eyes and visualize a serene place, such as a beach or forest. Engage all your senses to enhance the vividness of the image.

4. Incorporating These Techniques into Daily Life

- **Establishing a Routine:**
    - **Overview:** Incorporate mindfulness, meditation, and relaxation techniques into your daily routine to experience their full benefits.
    - **Recommendations:**
        - **Daily Practice:** Set aside time each day for mindfulness, meditation, or relaxation exercises, even if it's just for a few minutes.
        - **Consistent Schedule:** Aim for consistency in your practice to build a habit and integrate these techniques into your lifestyle.
- **Creating a Relaxing Environment:**
    - **Overview:** Designate a quiet, comfortable space for practicing mindfulness, meditation, and relaxation techniques.

- **Tips:**
  - **Comfortable Setting:** Choose a space with minimal distractions where you can sit or lie down comfortably.
  - **Ambient Conditions:** Use soft lighting, calming music, or essential oils to enhance the relaxation experience.

- **Using Technology:**
  - **Overview:** Utilize apps and online resources to support and guide your practice.
  - **Examples:**
    - **Meditation Apps:** Explore apps such as Headspace, Calm, or Insight Timer for guided meditation and relaxation exercises.
    - **Online Resources:** Access videos, podcasts, or online courses to learn and practice various techniques.

5. Benefits of Regular Practice

- **Enhanced Cognitive Function:**
  - **Overview:** Regular practice of mindfulness, meditation, and relaxation techniques can improve cognitive

function, including memory, attention, and executive function.

- **Improved Emotional Well-being:**
    - **Overview:** Supports emotional regulation, reduces symptoms of anxiety and depression, and promotes overall mental health.
- **Better Stress Management:**
    - **Overview:** Helps manage and reduce stress levels, leading to improved overall well-being and cognitive performance.

Developing Resilience Against Cognitive Decline

Resilience against cognitive decline involves adopting strategies and lifestyle changes that help maintain and even improve cognitive function as we age. This section explores ways to build cognitive resilience through proactive measures, personal habits, and lifestyle choices.

1. Understanding Cognitive Resilience

- **Definition:**
    - **Overview:** Cognitive resilience refers to the brain's ability to withstand and recover from challenges that threaten cognitive function, such as aging, stress, and neurological damage.

- **Purpose:** To maintain mental sharpness, adapt to changes, and recover from cognitive stressors effectively.

- **Key Components:**
    - **Neuroplasticity:** The brain's capacity to reorganize and adapt by forming new neural connections.
    - **Cognitive Reserve:** The brain's ability to use existing cognitive resources to compensate for damage or decline.

2. Strategies for Building Cognitive Resilience

- **Healthy Lifestyle Choices:**
    - **Balanced Diet:**
        - **Overview:** A nutrient-rich diet supports brain health and cognitive function.
        - **Recommendations:** Incorporate foods high in antioxidants, omega-3 fatty acids, and vitamins, such as fruits, vegetables, nuts, and fish.
        - **Examples:** Berries, leafy greens, fatty fish, and nuts.
    - **Regular Physical Exercise:**
        - **Overview:** Exercise improves blood flow to the brain, supports neurogenesis, and reduces the risk of cognitive decline.

- **Recommendations:** Engage in a mix of aerobic exercises, strength training, and balance activities.
- **Examples:** Walking, jogging, cycling, and resistance training.

  o **Quality Sleep:**
  - **Overview:** Adequate sleep is crucial for cognitive health, memory consolidation, and overall brain function.
  - **Recommendations:** Aim for 7-9 hours of quality sleep per night and maintain a consistent sleep schedule.
  - **Tips:** Create a relaxing bedtime routine and a sleep-friendly environment.

- **Mental Stimulation:**

  o **Cognitive Challenges:**
  - **Overview:** Engaging in mentally stimulating activities helps strengthen cognitive skills and build resilience.
  - **Recommendations:** Participate in activities that challenge the brain, such as puzzles, games, and learning new skills.

- **Examples:** Crossword puzzles, chess, and language learning.
- **Lifelong Learning:**
  - **Overview:** Continued education and skill development support cognitive health and adaptability.
  - **Recommendations:** Pursue formal or informal education, hobbies, and new interests.
  - **Examples:** Online courses, workshops, and creative pursuits.

- **Stress Management:**
  - **Overview:** Effective stress management reduces the impact of stress on cognitive function and overall health.
  - **Techniques:**
    - **Mindfulness and Meditation:** Practice mindfulness and meditation to reduce stress and enhance mental clarity.
    - **Relaxation Techniques:** Use deep breathing, progressive muscle relaxation, and other techniques to manage stress.
  - **Social Engagement:**
    - **Overview:** Maintaining strong social connections supports

emotional well-being and cognitive function.

- **Recommendations:** Engage in social activities, build meaningful relationships, and participate in community events.
- **Examples:** Social clubs, volunteering, and spending time with family and friends.

3. Building Cognitive Resilience Through Habits

- **Daily Routine:**
  - **Overview:** Establishing a structured daily routine can help support cognitive function and resilience.
  - **Recommendations:** Include regular physical activity, mental stimulation, and relaxation in your daily schedule.

- **Goal Setting:**
  - **Overview:** Setting and pursuing personal goals can provide motivation and a sense of purpose, contributing to cognitive resilience.
  - **Recommendations:** Set achievable goals related to health, learning, and personal development.
  - **Examples:** Fitness goals, learning a new skill, or completing a creative project.

- **Adaptability and Flexibility:**
    - **Overview:** Developing adaptability helps manage changes and challenges, supporting cognitive resilience.
    - **Recommendations:** Embrace change, learn from experiences, and be open to new approaches and solutions.

4. Professional Support and Resources

- **Healthcare Providers:**
    - **Overview:** Regular check-ups and consultations with healthcare providers can help monitor cognitive health and address any concerns.
    - **Recommendations:** Schedule routine health assessments, cognitive screenings, and follow-up appointments as needed.
- **Cognitive Training Programs:**
    - **Overview:** Specialized programs and therapies can help enhance cognitive function and resilience.
    - **Recommendations:** Explore cognitive training programs, therapies, and interventions designed to support brain health.
- **Support Networks:**

- **Overview:** Engaging with support networks and organizations can provide additional resources and assistance.
- **Recommendations:** Connect with support groups, educational organizations, and community resources focused on cognitive health.

5. Monitoring and Adapting Strategies

- **Self-Assessment:**
  - **Overview:** Regularly assess cognitive function and well-being to identify areas for improvement.
  - **Recommendations:** Use self-assessment tools, track progress, and make adjustments to strategies as needed.

- **Feedback and Evaluation:**
  - **Overview:** Seek feedback from healthcare providers, family, and peers to evaluate the effectiveness of resilience-building strategies.
  - **Recommendations:** Adjust strategies based on feedback and personal experiences to optimize cognitive health.

Chapter 7: Sleep and Brain Function

How Sleep Affects Cognitive Health

Sleep is essential for maintaining optimal cognitive health. It influences various aspects of brain function, including memory consolidation, cognitive performance, emotional regulation, and overall brain health. This section explores the intricate relationship between sleep and cognitive health, detailing how sleep impacts different cognitive functions and the consequences of inadequate sleep.

1. Memory Consolidation

- **Overview:**
    - **Memory Formation:** Sleep plays a critical role in transferring information from short-term to long-term memory.
    - **Types of Memory Affected:**
        - **Declarative Memory:** Involves factual and episodic information, such as facts, events, and experiences.
        - **Procedural Memory:** Involves skills and habits, such as riding a bike or playing a musical instrument.

- **NREM Sleep and Memory:**
  - **Slow-Wave Sleep (SWS):** A key stage of NREM sleep that supports the consolidation of declarative memories. It helps reinforce and stabilize newly acquired information.
  - **Memory Integration:** During SWS, the brain replays and integrates experiences, facilitating long-term memory storage.

- **REM Sleep and Memory:**
  - **Dreaming and Memory Processing:** REM sleep is associated with the processing and integration of emotional and procedural memories.
  - **Emotional Regulation:** REM sleep helps in processing emotional experiences and consolidating emotional memories.

2. Cognitive Performance

- **Attention and Concentration:**
  - **Effects of Sleep Quality:** Adequate sleep enhances attention and concentration, allowing for better focus and cognitive performance.
  - **Sleep Deprivation:** Impairs attention, leading to reduced vigilance, increased distractibility, and difficulty maintaining concentration.

- **Executive Function:**

- **Overview:** Executive functions include planning, decision-making, problem-solving, and impulse control.
- **Impact of Sleep:** Good sleep supports executive function, enabling more effective planning and problem-solving abilities.
- **Sleep Deprivation:** Can lead to impaired judgment, reduced decision-making ability, and difficulties in organizing tasks.

- **Reaction Time:**
    - **Overview:** Sleep affects the speed at which the brain processes information and responds to stimuli.
    - **Sleep Deprivation:** Slows reaction times, increasing the risk of errors and accidents, especially in high-stakes situations like driving.

3. Emotional Regulation

- **Emotional Stability:**
    - **Role of Sleep:** Quality sleep supports emotional stability by regulating mood and reducing emotional reactivity.
    - **Sleep Deprivation:** Leads to increased irritability, heightened emotional sensitivity, and difficulty managing stress.
- **Stress Management:**

- **Overview:** Adequate sleep helps the brain manage stress and recover from daily challenges.
- **Impact of Sleep Loss:** Chronic sleep deprivation can exacerbate stress and contribute to feelings of anxiety and depression.

- **Emotional Memory Processing:**
  - **Overview:** REM sleep plays a role in processing and integrating emotional experiences.
  - **Impact of Sleep Deprivation:** Impaired REM sleep can affect emotional memory processing, leading to difficulties in managing emotions and stress.

4. Brain Health and Neurodegenerative Diseases

- **Long-Term Brain Health:**
  - **Overview:** Quality sleep supports overall brain health and reduces the risk of neurodegenerative diseases.
  - **Sleep and Cognitive Decline:** Chronic sleep disturbances and insufficient sleep are associated with increased risk of cognitive decline and neurodegenerative conditions.

- **Alzheimer's Disease:**

- **Overview:** Research suggests a link between sleep disorders and an increased risk of Alzheimer's disease.
- **Mechanisms:** Sleep disturbances may contribute to the accumulation of beta-amyloid plaques and tau tangles, key features of Alzheimer's disease.

- **Parkinson's Disease:**
    - **Overview:** Poor sleep quality is also linked to Parkinson's disease, affecting motor function and cognitive abilities.
    - **Sleep Disruptions:** Can exacerbate motor symptoms and contribute to cognitive decline in Parkinson's patients.

5. Consequences of Inadequate Sleep

- **Short-Term Effects:**
    - **Cognitive Impairment:** Immediate impacts include reduced attention, impaired memory, and decreased cognitive performance.
    - **Emotional Instability:** Increased irritability and difficulty managing emotions.
- **Long-Term Effects:**
    - **Cognitive Decline:** Chronic sleep deprivation can contribute to long-term cognitive decline and an increased risk of neurodegenerative diseases.

- **Mental Health Issues:** Increased risk of developing anxiety, depression, and other mental health disorders.

6. Improving Sleep for Better Cognitive Health

- **Establishing a Sleep Routine:**
    - **Overview:** Consistent sleep routines support better sleep quality and cognitive function.
    - **Recommendations:** Go to bed and wake up at the same time each day, even on weekends.

- **Creating a Sleep-Friendly Environment:**
    - **Overview:** A conducive sleep environment enhances sleep quality.
    - **Recommendations:** Ensure a comfortable mattress, a cool room temperature, and minimal noise and light.

- **Addressing Sleep Disorders:**
    - **Overview:** Identifying and treating sleep disorders can improve sleep quality and cognitive health.
    - **Recommendations:** Seek professional help for conditions such as insomnia, sleep apnea, and restless legs syndrome.

Tips for Improving Sleep Quality

Quality sleep is crucial for maintaining overall health and cognitive function. Implementing effective strategies to enhance sleep quality can lead to better rest, improved mood, and optimal cognitive performance. This section provides practical tips for creating a sleep-friendly environment, establishing healthy sleep habits, and addressing common sleep challenges.

1. Establish a Consistent Sleep Schedule

- **Regular Sleep and Wake Times:**
    - **Overview:** Going to bed and waking up at the same time every day helps regulate your body's internal clock.
    - **Recommendations:** Aim for 7-9 hours of sleep each night, and stick to your sleep schedule even on weekends.
- **Gradual Adjustments:**
    - **Overview:** If you need to change your sleep schedule, do so gradually to avoid disrupting your internal clock.
    - **Recommendations:** Adjust your bedtime and wake-up time by 15-30 minutes every few days.

2. Create a Sleep-Friendly Environment

- **Comfortable Bedding:**

- **Overview:** A comfortable mattress and pillows support restful sleep.
- **Recommendations:** Choose bedding that suits your comfort preferences and replace worn-out mattresses and pillows as needed.

- **Optimal Room Temperature:**
  - **Overview:** A cool, comfortable room temperature promotes better sleep.
  - **Recommendations:** Keep your bedroom temperature between 60-67°F (15-19°C).

- **Minimize Noise and Light:**
  - **Overview:** Reducing noise and light levels in your bedroom can improve sleep quality.
  - **Recommendations:**
    - **Use Earplugs:** To block out disruptive sounds.
    - **Darken the Room:** Use blackout curtains or an eye mask to block light.
    - **White Noise Machine:** To mask background noise.

3. Develop a Relaxing Bedtime Routine

- **Wind Down Before Bed:**

- **Overview:** A relaxing pre-sleep routine helps signal to your body that it's time to wind down.
- **Recommendations:**
  - **Read a Book:** Choose calming, non-stimulating material.
  - **Take a Warm Bath:** Helps relax muscles and prepare for sleep.
  - **Practice Relaxation Techniques:** Try deep breathing, meditation, or gentle stretching.

- **Avoid Stimulating Activities:**
  - **Overview:** Engaging in stimulating activities before bed can interfere with your ability to fall asleep.
  - **Recommendations:**
    - **Limit Screen Time:** Avoid screens (phones, tablets, computers) at least an hour before bed due to blue light exposure.
    - **Avoid Heavy Meals and Caffeine:** Refrain from eating large meals, caffeine, or alcohol close to bedtime.

4. Manage Stress and Anxiety

- **Stress Reduction Techniques:**

- o **Overview:** Managing stress and anxiety can improve sleep quality.
- o **Recommendations:**
    - **Mindfulness and Meditation:** Practice mindfulness or meditation techniques to calm your mind.
    - **Journaling:** Write down thoughts or worries before bed to clear your mind.
- **Create a Worry-Free Zone:**
    - o **Overview:** Reserve your bedroom for sleep and relaxation to strengthen the association between the space and rest.
    - o **Recommendations:**
        - **Avoid Work or Stressful Activities:** Keep work, stressful tasks, and discussions out of the bedroom.

5. Maintain Healthy Lifestyle Habits

- **Regular Physical Activity:**
    - o **Overview:** Regular exercise supports better sleep and overall health.
    - o **Recommendations:** Engage in moderate physical activity for at least 30 minutes most days of the week, but avoid vigorous exercise close to bedtime.

- **Balanced Diet:**
    - **Overview:** A healthy diet supports better sleep and overall well-being.
    - **Recommendations:**
        - **Eat a Light Evening Snack:** If needed, opt for a light snack that promotes sleep, such as a small serving of yogurt or a banana.
        - **Avoid Heavy Meals and Excessive Fluids:** Refrain from eating large meals or drinking excessive fluids before bed to prevent discomfort and nighttime awakenings.

6. Address Common Sleep Challenges

- **Insomnia:**
    - **Overview:** Difficulty falling or staying asleep may indicate insomnia.
    - **Recommendations:** Implement sleep hygiene practices, consult a healthcare provider if insomnia persists, and explore cognitive behavioral therapy for insomnia (CBT-I) if needed.
- **Sleep Apnea:**
    - **Overview:** Sleep apnea is a condition where breathing repeatedly stops and starts during sleep.

- o **Recommendations:** Seek medical evaluation if you experience symptoms such as loud snoring, choking during sleep, or excessive daytime sleepiness.

- **Restless Legs Syndrome:**

    - o **Overview:** Restless legs syndrome involves uncomfortable sensations in the legs, leading to an urge to move them.

    - o **Recommendations:** Consult a healthcare provider for diagnosis and management strategies, which may include lifestyle changes or medication.

7. Seek Professional Help When Needed

- **Sleep Specialists:**

    - o **Overview:** Professionals specializing in sleep disorders can provide diagnosis and treatment.

    - o **Recommendations:** Consult a sleep specialist if you experience persistent sleep problems or disorders.

- **Cognitive Behavioral Therapy for Insomnia (CBT-I):**

    - o **Overview:** CBT-I is an evidence-based therapy that helps address insomnia by changing thoughts and behaviors related to sleep.

    - o **Recommendations:** Consider CBT-I if insomnia is affecting your quality of life and traditional sleep strategies have not been effective.

Understanding Sleep Disorders and Their Impact on the Brain

Sleep disorders can significantly affect cognitive function and overall brain health. This section explores various common sleep disorders, their symptoms, how they impact the brain, and strategies for managing these conditions to improve sleep quality and cognitive health.

1. Common Sleep Disorders

- **Insomnia:**
    - **Overview:** Insomnia involves difficulty falling asleep, staying asleep, or waking up too early and not being able to return to sleep.
    - **Symptoms:** Difficulty initiating or maintaining sleep, waking up feeling unrefreshed, daytime fatigue.
    - **Impact on the Brain:** Chronic insomnia can impair cognitive function, including attention, memory, and executive function. It is also linked to increased risk of mood disorders such as depression and anxiety.
- **Sleep Apnea:**

- - **Overview:** Sleep apnea is characterized by repeated interruptions in breathing during sleep, leading to fragmented sleep.
  - **Symptoms:** Loud snoring, choking or gasping during sleep, excessive daytime sleepiness, difficulty concentrating.
  - **Impact on the Brain:** Repeated oxygen deprivation and fragmented sleep can lead to cognitive impairment, memory problems, and increased risk of cardiovascular and metabolic conditions.

- **Restless Legs Syndrome (RLS):**
  - **Overview:** RLS involves uncomfortable sensations in the legs and an uncontrollable urge to move them, particularly at night.
  - **Symptoms:** Sensations of crawling, tingling, or itching in the legs, worsening symptoms at rest or in the evening, relief through movement.
  - **Impact on the Brain:** RLS can disrupt sleep continuity, leading to daytime sleepiness, impaired cognitive function, and decreased quality of life.

- **Narcolepsy:**
  - **Overview:** Narcolepsy is a chronic sleep disorder characterized by excessive daytime sleepiness and sudden sleep attacks.

- **Symptoms:** Excessive daytime sleepiness, cataplexy (sudden loss of muscle tone triggered by emotions), sleep paralysis, vivid hallucinations.
- **Impact on the Brain:** Narcolepsy can affect cognitive function, including attention, memory, and executive function. It may also lead to difficulties in maintaining consistent sleep patterns.

- **Circadian Rhythm Disorders:**
    - **Overview:** These disorders involve disruptions in the body's internal clock, affecting sleep-wake cycles.
    - **Types:** Includes delayed sleep phase disorder (sleeping late and waking up late) and advanced sleep phase disorder (sleeping early and waking up early).
    - **Impact on the Brain:** Disruptions in circadian rhythms can affect cognitive performance, mood regulation, and overall health. It may also lead to sleep deprivation and associated cognitive impairments.

2. How Sleep Disorders Affect Cognitive Function

- **Cognitive Impairment:**
    - **Overview:** Sleep disorders can lead to deficits in attention, memory, and cognitive performance.

- o **Mechanisms:** Fragmented sleep, reduced sleep duration, and insufficient deep sleep can impair cognitive processes and memory consolidation.

- **Emotional Regulation:**
    - o **Overview:** Sleep disorders can impact emotional stability and increase susceptibility to mood disorders.
    - o **Mechanisms:** Disrupted sleep can lead to increased emotional reactivity, mood swings, and higher risk of depression and anxiety.

- **Executive Function:**
    - o **Overview:** Executive functions such as decision-making, problem-solving, and planning may be compromised.
    - o **Mechanisms:** Impaired sleep quality affects the prefrontal cortex, which is responsible for executive functions and cognitive control.

- **Daytime Sleepiness and Fatigue:**
    - o **Overview:** Persistent daytime sleepiness and fatigue due to sleep disorders can impair daily functioning and productivity.
    - o **Mechanisms:** Reduced overall sleep quality and quantity lead to decreased alertness and cognitive efficiency.

3. Diagnosing Sleep Disorders

- **Sleep Studies:**
  - **Overview:** Sleep studies, including polysomnography and home sleep apnea testing, are used to diagnose sleep disorders.
  - **Types:**
    - **Polysomnography:** A comprehensive sleep study conducted in a sleep clinic to monitor brain waves, heart rate, and breathing during sleep.
    - **Home Sleep Apnea Testing:** A portable device used to diagnose sleep apnea by monitoring breathing patterns and oxygen levels at home.
- **Consulting a Sleep Specialist:**
  - **Overview:** A sleep specialist can provide diagnosis and treatment for sleep disorders.
  - **Recommendations:** Seek a sleep specialist if you experience persistent sleep issues or symptoms of sleep disorders.

4. Managing Sleep Disorders
- **Lifestyle Modifications:**

- **Overview:** Implementing lifestyle changes can improve sleep quality and manage symptoms of sleep disorders.
- **Recommendations:** Practice good sleep hygiene, establish a consistent sleep routine, and avoid stimulants and large meals close to bedtime.

- **Medical Treatments:**
    - **Overview:** Various medical treatments are available for managing sleep disorders.
    - **Types:**
        - **Medications:** Prescription medications, such as sleep aids or medications for specific sleep disorders (e.g., CPAP for sleep apnea).
        - **Behavioral Therapies:** Cognitive Behavioral Therapy for Insomnia (CBT-I) can be effective for managing insomnia.

- **Therapies and Interventions:**
    - **Overview:** Additional therapies may be used to address specific sleep disorders.
    - **Types:**
        - **Continuous Positive Airway Pressure (CPAP):** For managing

sleep apnea by keeping airways open during sleep.

- **Iron Supplements or Medication:** For managing Restless Legs Syndrome if associated with iron deficiency or other underlying conditions.

Chapter 8: Social Connections and Cognitive Health

The Role of Social Interaction in Preventing Cognitive Decline

Social interaction plays a significant role in maintaining cognitive health and preventing cognitive decline. Engaging in meaningful social activities and maintaining strong relationships can help support brain function, reduce the risk of cognitive disorders, and enhance overall well-being. This section explores how social interaction influences cognitive health and offers strategies for leveraging social connections to prevent cognitive decline.

1. How Social Interaction Supports Cognitive Function

- **Cognitive Stimulation:**
    - **Overview:** Engaging in social activities stimulates cognitive processes such as memory, attention, and problem-solving.
    - **Mechanisms:** Social interactions often involve complex communication, memory recall, and mental engagement, which contribute to cognitive stimulation and mental agility.

- **Emotional and Psychological Benefits:**
    - **Overview:** Positive social interactions help regulate emotions and reduce stress, which can impact cognitive health.
    - **Mechanisms:** Emotional support from social connections can buffer against stress and anxiety, both of which are linked to cognitive decline.
- **Social Engagement and Brain Health:**
    - **Overview:** Active social engagement is associated with lower risk of cognitive decline and dementia.
    - **Research Findings:** Studies have shown that individuals with robust social networks and frequent social interactions have a lower risk of developing cognitive disorders and experience slower cognitive decline.

2. Research Evidence on Social Interaction and Cognitive Decline

- **Longitudinal Studies:**
    - **Overview:** Long-term studies track the effects of social engagement on cognitive health over time.
    - **Findings:** Research indicates that individuals with strong social networks and frequent social interactions experience slower rates of cognitive

decline and a lower incidence of dementia.

- **Cross-Sectional Studies:**
  - **Overview:** Studies comparing cognitive health among individuals with varying levels of social engagement.
  - **Findings:** Higher levels of social engagement are associated with better cognitive function and reduced risk of cognitive impairment.

- **Experimental Studies:**
  - **Overview:** Interventions designed to increase social interaction and their effects on cognitive health.
  - **Findings:** Programs that promote social participation, such as community activities or group therapies, have demonstrated positive effects on cognitive function and overall well-being.

3. Strategies for Enhancing Social Interaction

- **Participate in Group Activities:**
  - **Overview:** Engaging in group activities provides opportunities for social interaction and cognitive stimulation.
  - **Recommendations:**
    - **Join Clubs or Organizations:** Participate in community clubs,

hobby groups, or social organizations that interest you.

- **Attend Social Events:** Regularly attend social gatherings, community events, or cultural activities.

- **Maintain Regular Contact with Loved Ones:**
  - **Overview:** Keeping in touch with family and friends supports social bonds and cognitive health.
  - **Recommendations:**
    - **Schedule Regular Visits:** Plan regular get-togethers with family and friends.
    - **Use Technology:** Stay connected through phone calls, video chats, and social media.

- **Engage in Volunteer Work:**
  - **Overview:** Volunteering provides a sense of purpose and opportunities for social engagement.
  - **Recommendations:** Volunteer for causes you care about and seek out community service opportunities.

- **Join Support Groups:**

- **Overview:** Support groups offer a space to share experiences and receive emotional support.
- **Recommendations:** Join support groups related to personal interests, health conditions, or life stages.

4. Addressing Social Isolation

- **Recognizing Social Isolation:**
  - **Overview:** Social isolation can contribute to cognitive decline and poor mental health.
  - **Indicators:** Limited social interactions, feelings of loneliness, and lack of meaningful connections.

- **Strategies to Combat Isolation:**
  - **Overview:** Implementing strategies to increase social interactions and reduce feelings of isolation.
  - **Recommendations:**
    - **Reach Out for Support:** Seek help from social services, community organizations, or mental health professionals if experiencing isolation.
    - **Pursue New Social Opportunities:** Explore new activities or groups to expand your social network.

5. The Impact of Social Interaction on Specific Cognitive Functions

- **Memory and Learning:**
    - **Overview:** Social interactions often involve recalling past experiences and learning new information.
    - **Benefits:** Engaging in conversations and social activities can enhance memory and learning abilities.

- **Attention and Focus:**
    - **Overview:** Social interactions require attentiveness and focus.
    - **Benefits:** Regular social engagement can improve attention and concentration skills.

- **Problem-Solving and Decision-Making:**
    - **Overview:** Social interactions often involve collaborative problem-solving and decision-making.
    - **Benefits:** Participating in group discussions and collaborative activities can enhance these cognitive abilities.

6. Social Interaction Across the Lifespan

- **Childhood and Adolescence:**

- **Overview:** Social interactions play a critical role in cognitive and emotional development during early life.
- **Recommendations:** Encourage participation in social activities, team sports, and peer interactions.

- **Adulthood:**
  - **Overview:** Maintaining social connections through work, friendships, and community involvement supports cognitive health in adulthood.
  - **Recommendations:** Balance professional, personal, and social activities to sustain meaningful relationships.

- **Older Adults:**
  - **Overview:** Social engagement remains crucial in later life to support cognitive function and emotional well-being.
  - **Recommendations:** Stay active in social circles, participate in senior programs, and maintain regular contact with loved ones.

Building and Maintaining Strong Social Networks

Strong social networks are essential for cognitive health, emotional well-being, and overall life satisfaction. Building and maintaining meaningful relationships requires intentional effort and active participation. This section provides practical strategies for creating and nurturing strong social networks to support cognitive and emotional health.

1. **Understanding the Benefits of Strong Social Networks**

   - **Cognitive Health:**
     - **Overview:** Robust social networks provide cognitive stimulation and support mental agility.
     - **Benefits:** Regular interaction and engagement with others help keep the brain active and reduce the risk of cognitive decline.

   - **Emotional Well-Being:**
     - **Overview:** Strong social connections contribute to emotional stability and stress management.
     - **Benefits:** Supportive relationships can enhance mood, reduce feelings of loneliness, and provide a sense of belonging.

- **Overall Quality of Life:**
    - **Overview:** Social networks contribute to a richer, more fulfilling life experience.
    - **Benefits:** Increased social engagement is associated with higher life satisfaction and better overall health.

2. Strategies for Building Social Networks

- **Identify Your Interests and Passions:**
    - **Overview:** Engaging in activities that you enjoy can lead to meeting like-minded individuals.
    - **Recommendations:**
        - **Join Clubs and Organizations:** Participate in groups or clubs that align with your hobbies and interests.
        - **Attend Events and Workshops:** Attend local events, seminars, and workshops related to your interests.
- **Leverage Existing Connections:**
    - **Overview:** Use your current social circle to expand your network.
    - **Recommendations:**

- **Ask for Introductions:** Request friends or acquaintances to introduce you to new people.

- **Attend Social Gatherings:** Go to gatherings or parties hosted by friends to meet new individuals.

- **Volunteer and Get Involved:**
  - **Overview:** Volunteering provides opportunities to meet people while contributing to a cause.
  - **Recommendations:**
    - **Volunteer for Local Organizations:** Join volunteer programs or community service projects.
    - **Participate in Fundraising Events:** Get involved in fundraising activities for causes you care about.

- **Pursue Professional and Educational Opportunities:**
  - **Overview:** Professional and educational settings can be great places to build new connections.
  - **Recommendations:**
    - **Attend Conferences and Networking Events:** Participate in

industry conferences and professional networking events.

- **Enroll in Courses or Workshops:** Take courses or workshops to meet others with similar professional or educational goals.

3. Maintaining and Nurturing Relationships

- **Stay in Regular Contact:**
  - **Overview:** Consistent communication helps sustain relationships.
  - **Recommendations:**
    - **Schedule Regular Check-Ins:** Plan regular calls, messages, or visits with friends and family.
    - **Send Updates and Greetings:** Share updates about your life and send greetings for special occasions.

- **Be Supportive and Engaged:**
  - **Overview:** Showing support and being actively engaged in relationships strengthens bonds.
  - **Recommendations:**
    - **Offer Help and Encouragement:** Be there for friends and family during challenging times and celebrate their successes.

- **Engage in Meaningful Conversations:** Have deep and meaningful conversations to strengthen connections.

- **Resolve Conflicts and Address Issues:**
  - **Overview:** Addressing conflicts and issues promptly helps maintain healthy relationships.
  - **Recommendations:**
    - **Communicate Openly:** Discuss any concerns or misunderstandings directly and respectfully.
    - **Seek Compromise:** Work towards finding solutions that satisfy both parties and resolve conflicts amicably.

4. Expanding Your Social Network

- **Explore New Social Opportunities:**
  - **Overview:** Actively seeking out new social opportunities helps expand your network.
  - **Recommendations:**
    - **Join Online Communities:** Participate in online forums, groups, or social media platforms related to your interests.

- **Attend Meetups and Social Events:** Look for local meetups or social events that offer opportunities to meet new people.

- **Be Open to Diverse Connections:**
  - **Overview:** Building relationships with a diverse range of individuals enriches your social network.
  - **Recommendations:**
    - **Engage with Different Groups:** Connect with people from different backgrounds, cultures, and interests.
    - **Be Curious and Open-Minded:** Show interest in learning about others' experiences and perspectives.

5. Utilizing Technology to Maintain Connections

- **Digital Communication Tools:**
  - **Overview:** Technology offers various tools for maintaining and enhancing social connections.
  - **Recommendations:**
    - **Use Video Calls and Messaging Apps:** Stay in touch with friends and family using video calls, messaging apps, and social media platforms.

- **Participate in Online Groups:** Join online groups or forums related to your interests to connect with others virtually.

- **Balancing Online and Offline Interactions:**
  - **Overview:** While technology facilitates communication, balancing online interactions with in-person engagement is important.
  - **Recommendations:**
    - **Schedule Face-to-Face Meetings:** Plan regular in-person meetings or gatherings to complement online interactions.
    - **Engage in Local Activities:** Participate in local events and activities to strengthen real-world connections.

6. Building Social Networks in Different Life Stages

- **Young Adults:**
  - **Overview:** Building social networks during early adulthood sets the foundation for future relationships.
  - **Recommendations:** Engage in social and professional activities, and build connections through education and early career opportunities.
- **Middle Age:**

- o **Overview:** Maintaining and expanding social networks during middle age supports well-being and professional growth.
- o **Recommendations:** Balance work, family, and social activities to sustain and nurture relationships.

- **Later Life:**
  - o **Overview:** Social connections remain vital in later life to support cognitive health and emotional well-being.
  - o **Recommendations:** Stay active in social circles, participate in senior programs, and continue to seek out new opportunities for social engagement.

Activities and Communities That Promote Cognitive Engagement

Engaging in various activities and participating in community groups can significantly enhance cognitive function and overall brain health. This section explores different types of activities and communities that promote cognitive engagement, offering practical suggestions for incorporating them into daily life.

1. Cognitive-Stimulating Activities

- **Mental Challenges:**

- **Overview:** Activities that challenge the mind can improve cognitive function and mental agility.
- **Examples:**
  - **Puzzles and Brain Teasers:** Engage in crosswords, Sudoku, logic puzzles, and other brain teasers.
  - **Strategy Games:** Play chess, checkers, or other strategy-based games that require planning and critical thinking.

- **Learning and Skill Development:**
  - **Overview:** Learning new skills or acquiring knowledge stimulates cognitive processes.
  - **Examples:**
    - **Language Learning:** Study a new language to enhance memory and cognitive flexibility.
    - **Musical Instruments:** Learn to play an instrument, which involves memory, coordination, and auditory processing.

- **Creative Outlets:**
  - **Overview:** Creative activities stimulate various cognitive functions and provide emotional expression.

- Examples:
  - **Art and Craft Projects:** Engage in painting, drawing, sculpting, or other artistic endeavors.
  - **Writing and Journaling:** Practice writing, whether through creative writing, journaling, or blogging.

2. Social and Community-Based Activities

- **Participating in Clubs and Organizations:**
  - **Overview:** Joining clubs or organizations offers social interaction and cognitive stimulation.
  - **Examples:**
    - **Book Clubs:** Discuss books and literature with others to engage in critical thinking and social interaction.
    - **Hobby Groups:** Participate in groups focused on shared hobbies, such as gardening, photography, or cooking.

- **Volunteering and Community Service:**
  - **Overview:** Volunteering provides opportunities for social engagement and cognitive challenge.
  - **Examples:**

- **Community Projects:** Get involved in local community projects, such as organizing events or leading educational workshops.
- **Mentorship Programs:** Mentor others, which involves teaching and sharing knowledge, and can be intellectually stimulating.

- **Social Gatherings and Events:**
  - **Overview:** Attending social events and gatherings promotes social interaction and cognitive engagement.
  - **Examples:**
    - **Local Events:** Attend festivals, fairs, or cultural events to experience new things and interact with others.
    - **Networking Events:** Participate in professional or networking events to engage with people and exchange ideas.

3. Physical Activities with Cognitive Benefits

- **Exercise and Physical Fitness:**
  - **Overview:** Regular physical activity is linked to improved cognitive function and brain health.
  - **Examples:**

- **Aerobic Exercise:** Engage in activities like walking, running, cycling, or swimming to boost brain health and overall fitness.
- **Mind-Body Exercises:** Practice yoga, tai chi, or other exercises that combine physical movement with mental focus.

- **Dance and Movement:**
  - **Overview:** Dance and coordinated movement activities stimulate cognitive and physical coordination.
  - **Examples:**
    - **Dance Classes:** Join dance classes or groups to improve coordination, memory, and social interaction.
    - **Movement Workshops:** Participate in workshops that focus on body awareness and movement, such as improvisational dance.

4. Online and Virtual Communities

- **Online Learning Platforms:**
  - **Overview:** Virtual learning platforms provide access to educational content and cognitive stimulation.
  - **Examples:**

- **Online Courses:** Enroll in online courses or MOOCs (Massive Open Online Courses) to learn new subjects and skills.
- **Educational Webinars:** Attend webinars and virtual lectures on topics of interest.

- **Virtual Social Groups:**
  - **Overview:** Online social groups and forums offer opportunities for interaction and cognitive engagement.
  - **Examples:**
    - **Online Discussion Forums:** Join forums or discussion groups on topics of interest to engage in conversations and share knowledge.
    - **Virtual Book Clubs:** Participate in online book clubs to discuss literature and connect with others.

5. Lifelong Learning and Continuing Education

- **Adult Education Programs:**
  - **Overview:** Continuing education programs offer opportunities for learning and cognitive engagement.
  - **Examples:**

- **Community College Classes:** Enroll in classes at local community colleges or adult education centers.
- **Workshops and Seminars:** Attend workshops and seminars on various topics to expand your knowledge.

- Educational and Cultural Institutions:
  - **Overview:** Museums, libraries, and cultural institutions provide educational experiences and cognitive stimulation.
  - **Examples:**
    - **Museum Visits:** Explore museums and exhibitions to learn about history, art, and science.
    - **Library Programs:** Participate in library programs, such as lectures, book readings, and educational events.

6. Engaging in Cognitive Health Programs

- **Brain Health Programs:**
  - **Overview:** Programs specifically designed to promote brain health and cognitive function.
  - **Examples:**

- **Cognitive Training Programs:** Engage in programs that offer exercises and activities to enhance cognitive abilities.
- **Brain Health Workshops:** Attend workshops focused on strategies for maintaining and improving brain health.

- **Support Groups and Cognitive Health Initiatives:**
    - **Overview:** Support groups and initiatives provide resources and community for cognitive health.
    - **Examples:**
        - **Support Groups for Cognitive Health:** Join groups focused on brain health, memory, and cognitive function.
        - **Health Initiatives:** Participate in community health initiatives that promote cognitive wellness.

Chapter 9: Brain Health and Technology

The Benefits and Risks of Technology on Cognitive Health

Technology has a profound impact on cognitive health, offering various benefits but also presenting certain risks. Understanding these can help individuals make informed decisions about incorporating technology into their cognitive health strategies.

Benefits of Technology on Cognitive Health

1. **Enhanced Cognitive Training and Mental Stimulation:**
    - **Overview:** Technology provides a range of tools and apps designed to enhance cognitive function and mental stimulation.
    - **Examples:**
        - **Brain Training Apps:** Applications like Lumosity and CogniFit offer exercises to improve memory, attention, and problem-solving skills.
        - **Educational Platforms:** Online courses and learning platforms provide opportunities for

continuous mental engagement and skill development.

2. **Convenience and Accessibility:**
   - **Overview:** Technology makes cognitive health resources more accessible and convenient.
   - **Examples:**
     - **Telemedicine:** Allows for remote consultations with healthcare professionals, making it easier to manage cognitive health from home.
     - **Mental Health Apps:** Provide on-the-go access to mental health resources, including mood tracking and relaxation exercises.

3. **Personalization and Adaptation:**
   - **Overview:** Many technology solutions can be personalized to individual needs, enhancing their effectiveness.
   - **Examples:**
     - **AI-Powered Tools:** Use artificial intelligence to adapt cognitive training programs to individual progress and needs.
     - **Wearable Devices:** Monitor health metrics and provide

personalized recommendations for improving cognitive function.

4. **Support for Cognitive Rehabilitation and Therapy:**
   - **Overview:** Technology can support cognitive rehabilitation and therapeutic interventions.
   - **Examples:**
     - **Virtual Reality (VR):** Offers immersive environments for cognitive rehabilitation and therapy.
     - **Cognitive Behavioral Therapy (CBT) Apps:** Provide structured CBT programs to address cognitive and emotional challenges.

5. **Increased Opportunities for Social Interaction:**
   - **Overview:** Technology facilitates social connections and engagement, which are beneficial for cognitive health.
   - **Examples:**
     - **Social Media:** Helps maintain connections with friends and family, reducing feelings of isolation.
     - **Online Communities:** Provides platforms for interacting with

others who share similar interests or experiences.

Risks of Technology on Cognitive Health

1. **Overreliance and Dependence:**
   - **Overview:** Excessive use of technology can lead to overreliance and dependency, potentially impacting cognitive health negatively.
   - **Examples:**
     - **Reduced Critical Thinking:** Overreliance on digital tools may reduce the need for active problem-solving and critical thinking.
     - **Cognitive Load:** Constant notifications and multitasking can increase cognitive load and reduce focus.

2. **Privacy and Security Concerns:**
   - **Overview:** The use of technology raises concerns about privacy and data security, which can impact cognitive health indirectly.
   - **Examples:**
     - **Data Breaches:** Risks of personal data being compromised or misused.

- **Privacy Issues:** Concerns about the collection and use of personal health data by technology providers.

3. **Potential Negative Impact on Sleep and Mental Health:**
   - **Overview:** Technology use, particularly before bedtime, can negatively affect sleep and mental health.
   - **Examples:**
     - **Blue Light Exposure:** The blue light emitted by screens can interfere with sleep patterns and circadian rhythms.
     - **Screen Time and Anxiety:** Excessive screen time can contribute to increased anxiety and stress levels.

4. **Quality and Effectiveness of Digital Tools:**
   - **Overview:** Not all technology solutions are created equal, and some may lack scientific validation.
   - **Examples:**
     - **Unproven Claims:** Some cognitive training apps and health tools may make unverified claims about their effectiveness.

- **Inconsistent Results:** Variability in the quality and effectiveness of digital health interventions.

5. **Social Isolation and Reduced Face-to-Face Interaction:**
    - **Overview:** Heavy reliance on digital communication can reduce opportunities for face-to-face social interaction, impacting cognitive and emotional health.
    - **Examples:**
        - **Decreased In-Person Social Engagement:** Reduced participation in real-world social activities and interactions.
        - **Impact on Social Skills:** Potential decline in social skills and interpersonal communication due to increased reliance on digital interactions.

Balancing the Benefits and Risks

1. **Moderation and Mindful Use:**
    - **Overview:** To maximize benefits and minimize risks, use technology mindfully and in moderation.
    - **Strategies:**
        - **Set Boundaries:** Establish limits on screen time and technology use to avoid overreliance.

- **Prioritize Face-to-Face Interaction:** Balance digital communication with in-person social activities.

2. **Evaluate and Choose Quality Tools:**
   - **Overview:** Select technology tools that are evidence-based and have proven efficacy.
   - **Strategies:**
     - **Research and Reviews:** Look for tools with positive reviews and scientific backing.
     - **Consult Professionals:** Seek recommendations from healthcare professionals for reliable and effective tools.

3. **Protect Privacy and Security:**
   - **Overview:** Implement measures to safeguard personal data and privacy when using technology.
   - **Strategies:**
     - **Use Secure Platforms:** Choose technology providers with strong security practices.
     - **Be Cautious with Data Sharing:** Limit the amount of personal information shared online and review privacy settings.

4. **Promote Balanced Use of Technology:**
    - **Overview:** Integrate technology into a balanced lifestyle that includes physical activity, social interaction, and mental engagement.
    - **Strategies:**
        - **Combine with Offline Activities:** Engage in non-digital activities that promote cognitive and emotional well-being.
        - **Monitor and Adjust Use:** Regularly assess the impact of technology on your cognitive health and make adjustments as needed.

Balancing Screen Time and Cognitive Engagement

In the digital age, managing screen time is crucial for maintaining cognitive health and overall well-being. While technology can offer valuable tools for cognitive engagement, excessive screen time can lead to negative effects. This section explores strategies for balancing screen time with other forms of cognitive engagement to optimize brain health.

1. Understanding the Impact of Screen Time on Cognitive Health

- **Positive Aspects:**

- - Educational and Cognitive Benefits: Screen time can provide access to educational content, cognitive training apps, and virtual social interactions.
  - Convenience: Technology offers convenience for accessing information, engaging in online learning, and staying connected with others.
- Negative Aspects:
  - Cognitive Overload: Prolonged screen time can contribute to cognitive overload, affecting focus, attention, and mental clarity.
  - Reduced Face-to-Face Interaction: Excessive screen use may reduce opportunities for in-person social interactions, impacting social skills and emotional health.
  - Physical Effects: Extended screen time can lead to physical issues such as eye strain, poor posture, and disrupted sleep patterns.

2. Setting Healthy Screen Time Limits

- **Establishing Guidelines:**
  - **Daily Limits:** Set specific daily limits for screen time based on age, activity, and individual needs.

- - **Breaks and Rest Periods:** Incorporate regular breaks and rest periods to reduce eye strain and prevent cognitive fatigue.
- **Creating Screen-Free Zones:**
  - **Designated Areas:** Establish areas in the home where screens are not allowed, such as the dining room or bedroom.
  - **Screen-Free Times:** Designate certain times of the day, such as during meals or before bedtime, as screen-free periods.
- **Monitoring and Tracking:**
  - **Screen Time Tracking:** Use apps or built-in features on devices to monitor and track screen time usage.
  - **Regular Reviews:** Periodically review screen time habits and make adjustments as needed to stay within healthy limits.

3. Incorporating Non-Screen Cognitive Activities

- **Engaging in Offline Learning:**
  - **Books and Magazines:** Read physical books and magazines to stimulate the mind and reduce screen dependency.
  - **Educational Workshops:** Attend in-person workshops, lectures, or classes for interactive learning experiences.
- **Participating in Brain-Boosting Hobbies:**

- - **Creative Arts:** Engage in creative activities such as painting, drawing, or crafting that do not involve screens.
  - **Puzzles and Games:** Solve puzzles, play board games, or participate in other non-digital activities that challenge the mind.
- **Physical Exercise and Movement:**
  - **Outdoor Activities:** Take part in outdoor activities such as walking, hiking, or sports to promote physical and cognitive health.
  - **Mind-Body Exercises:** Practice yoga, tai chi, or other exercises that combine physical movement with mental focus.

4. Enhancing Social Interaction Beyond Screens

- **Fostering In-Person Connections:**
  - **Social Gatherings:** Participate in social gatherings, clubs, or community events to build and maintain face-to-face relationships.
  - **Volunteering:** Get involved in volunteer activities to connect with others and contribute to the community.
- **Maintaining Strong Relationships:**
  - **Regular Meetups:** Schedule regular in-person meetups with friends and family to strengthen social bonds.

- - ○ **Quality Time:** Focus on quality interactions and meaningful conversations during in-person meetings.

5. Integrating Technology Mindfully

- **Purposeful Use of Technology:**
    - ○ **Intentional Engagement:** Use technology with specific goals in mind, such as educational purposes or productivity, rather than passive consumption.
    - ○ **Balanced Approach:** Balance technology use with other cognitive and physical activities to avoid overreliance.

- **Choosing Quality Content:**
    - ○ **Educational and Enriching Content:** Opt for content that is educational, enriching, and aligned with cognitive health goals.
    - ○ **Avoiding Mindless Scrolling:** Limit time spent on activities like social media or news consumption that may contribute to cognitive fatigue.

6. Developing Healthy Digital Habits

- **Mindful Consumption:**
    - ○ **Active Engagement:** Engage with digital content actively by taking notes, summarizing information, or discussing topics with others.

- **Reflection:** Reflect on digital experiences and assess their impact on cognitive health and overall well-being.

- **Creating a Balanced Routine:**
  - **Daily Schedule:** Incorporate a balanced routine that includes a mix of screen time, physical activity, social interaction, and cognitive exercises.
  - **Personalized Approach:** Tailor the routine to individual preferences and needs to maintain a healthy balance.

7. Evaluating and Adjusting Screen Time Practices

- **Regular Assessment:**
  - **Self-Evaluation:** Periodically assess screen time habits and their impact on cognitive health and well-being.
  - **Feedback from Others:** Seek feedback from family, friends, or healthcare professionals on screen time practices and make adjustments as needed.

- **Adapting to Changes:**
  - **Flexible Adjustments:** Be flexible and willing to adjust screen time practices based on changes in lifestyle, work, or personal circumstances.
  - **Staying Informed:** Stay informed about new research and guidelines related to screen time and cognitive health.

Chapter 10: Early Signs of Cognitive Decline and What to Do

Recognizing the Early Signs of Cognitive Decline

Early recognition of cognitive decline is essential for timely intervention and effective management. This section explores common early signs of cognitive decline and how to identify them to take appropriate action.

1. Memory Problems

- **Frequent Forgetfulness:**
    - **Description:** Regularly forgetting recent events, appointments, or conversations that one would normally remember.
    - **Examples:**
        - Forgetting to take medications or attend scheduled appointments.
        - Repeating questions or stories within a short period.
- **Difficulty Retaining New Information:**

- **Description:** Struggling to learn and remember new information or instructions.
- **Examples:**
  - Trouble remembering names, places, or new procedures.
  - Difficulty following a series of instructions or remembering recent changes in routines.

2. Difficulty with Daily Tasks

- **Trouble Organizing Tasks:**
  - **Description:** Difficulty planning, organizing, or completing daily tasks and activities.
  - **Examples:**
    - Problems with managing finances or organizing household chores.
    - Difficulty creating and following a to-do list or managing time effectively.

- **Misplacing Items:**
  - **Description:** Frequently losing or misplacing everyday items, which can lead to confusion and frustration.
  - **Examples:**

- Regularly misplacing keys, glasses, or other commonly used items.
- Difficulty retracing steps to find lost items.

3. Confusion and Disorientation

- **Getting Lost:**
    - **Description:** Becoming disoriented in familiar places or having trouble following a route.
    - **Examples:**
        - Getting lost in previously familiar environments, such as one's own neighborhood.
        - Difficulty finding one's way back to a familiar location or navigating through familiar routes.

- **Difficulty Understanding Time and Dates:**
    - **Description:** Confusing dates, times, or events, leading to disorientation and scheduling issues.
    - **Examples:**
        - Not knowing what day it is or forgetting important dates like birthdays or anniversaries.

- Confusing past and future events or not understanding the sequence of events.

4. Language and Communication Issues

- **Difficulty Finding Words:**
  - **Description:** Struggling to find the right words or using incorrect words in conversation.
  - **Examples:**
    - Having trouble recalling specific words or names during conversations.
    - Using vague or incorrect words, leading to confusion or misunderstandings.

- **Repeating Stories:**
  - **Description:** Repeating the same stories or questions, often within a short time frame.
  - **Examples:**
    - Telling the same story multiple times to the same audience.
    - Asking the same questions repeatedly, even after receiving answers.

5. Changes in Judgment and Decision-Making

- **Poor Decision-Making:**
  - **Description:** Making unusual or poor decisions that deviate from one's typical behavior.
  - **Examples:**
    - Making financially irresponsible decisions, such as excessive spending or poor investments.
    - Engaging in risky behaviors or making decisions without considering potential consequences.
- **Difficulty Problem-Solving:**
  - **Description:** Struggling with problem-solving or reasoning tasks, leading to difficulties in everyday activities.
  - **Examples:**
    - Difficulty solving simple problems or completing tasks that were previously manageable.
    - Trouble following logical steps to resolve issues or make decisions.

6. Changes in Mood and Behavior

- **Unusual Mood Swings:**

- **Description:** Experiencing frequent mood swings, irritability, or emotional outbursts that are out of character.
- **Examples:**
  - Sudden and unexplained changes in mood, such as becoming unusually angry or upset.
  - Emotional responses that are disproportionate to the situation or context.

- **Withdrawal from Social Activities:**
  - **Description:** Avoiding social interactions or becoming disengaged from previously enjoyed activities.
  - **Examples:**
    - Stopping participation in social events, hobbies, or community activities.
    - Isolating oneself from friends and family or declining invitations to social gatherings.

7. Monitoring and Documentation

- **Keeping Track of Changes:**
  - **Description:** Monitoring and documenting any cognitive changes or symptoms over time.

- Examples:
  - Maintaining a journal to record memory lapses, difficulties with daily tasks, and changes in behavior.
  - Using checklists or digital tools to track cognitive symptoms and their frequency.
- **Seeking Feedback from Others:**
  - **Description:** Getting input from family members, friends, or caregivers about observed changes in cognitive function.
  - **Examples:**
    - Asking loved ones for their observations and feedback regarding any cognitive changes.
    - Sharing concerns with others who may have noticed similar issues.

8. When to Seek Professional Help

- **Consulting Healthcare Professionals:**
  - **Description:** Seeking evaluation from healthcare providers if early signs of cognitive decline are observed.
  - **Examples:**
    - Scheduling an appointment with a primary care physician or a

> specialist, such as a neurologist or geriatrician.
>
> - Discussing symptoms and concerns with a healthcare provider for further assessment and diagnosis.

- **Utilizing Diagnostic Tools:**
  - **Description:** Considering the use of diagnostic tools and assessments to evaluate cognitive function.
  - **Examples:**
    - Undergoing neuropsychological testing to assess memory, attention, and other cognitive functions.
    - Exploring imaging techniques like MRI or CT scans if recommended by a healthcare provider.

Steps to Take When You Notice Changes

When you observe signs of cognitive decline, taking proactive steps is crucial for managing the situation effectively and ensuring timely intervention. This section outlines practical steps to take when you notice changes in cognitive function.

1. Document the Changes

- **Keep a Detailed Record:**
    - **Description:** Maintain a journal or log to document specific changes in cognitive function, including the frequency, severity, and impact of symptoms.
    - **Examples:** Record instances of memory lapses, difficulties with daily tasks, and changes in mood or behavior.
- **Track Patterns and Triggers:**
    - **Description:** Identify any patterns or potential triggers that may influence cognitive changes.
    - **Examples:** Note if changes occur during certain times of day, in response to specific events, or after particular activities.

2. Evaluate the Impact

- **Assess Daily Functioning:**
    - **Description:** Evaluate how the cognitive changes are affecting daily life, work, and social interactions.
    - **Examples:** Determine if changes are impacting the ability to perform routine tasks, maintain employment, or engage in social activities.
- **Consider Quality of Life:**

- Description: Reflect on how cognitive changes are influencing overall quality of life and emotional well-being.
- Examples: Assess feelings of frustration, anxiety, or depression related to cognitive difficulties.

3. Communicate with Others

- **Talk to Family and Friends:**
  - **Description:** Share observations and concerns with family members, friends, or trusted individuals who may have noticed similar changes.
  - **Examples:** Discuss cognitive changes openly with loved ones to gain their perspective and support.

- **Seek Input from Caregivers:**
  - **Description:** If applicable, involve caregivers or support providers in discussions about cognitive changes and their impact.
  - **Examples:** Share information with caregivers to ensure they are aware of any changes and can provide appropriate support.

4. Consult Healthcare Professionals

- **Schedule a Medical Evaluation:**

- - **Description:** Make an appointment with a healthcare provider for a comprehensive evaluation of cognitive function.
  - **Examples:** Consult a primary care physician, neurologist, or geriatrician for a thorough assessment.
- **Undergo Diagnostic Testing:**
  - **Description:** Consider undergoing diagnostic tests, such as neuropsychological assessments, brain imaging, or lab tests, as recommended by the healthcare provider.
  - **Examples:** Participate in cognitive tests to evaluate memory, attention, and other cognitive functions.

5. Explore Treatment and Management Options

- **Discuss Treatment Options:**
  - **Description:** Review potential treatment and management options with healthcare professionals based on the evaluation and diagnosis.
  - **Examples:** Explore options such as medication, cognitive therapies, or lifestyle changes to address cognitive decline.
- **Implement Management Strategies:**

- Description: Begin implementing recommended strategies or interventions to manage cognitive changes and support brain health.
- Examples: Follow prescribed treatments, engage in cognitive exercises, and adopt healthy lifestyle habits.

6. Seek Support and Resources

- **Join Support Groups:**
  - **Description:** Consider joining support groups or networks for individuals and families affected by cognitive decline or dementia.
  - **Examples:** Participate in local or online support groups to connect with others facing similar challenges.

- **Utilize Educational Resources:**
  - **Description:** Access educational resources, including books, websites, and organizations, to learn more about cognitive health and management strategies.
  - **Examples:** Use resources from reputable organizations such as the Alzheimer's Association or local dementia support services.

7. Plan for the Future

- **Create a Care Plan:**

- - **Description:** Develop a personalized care plan that outlines strategies for managing cognitive decline and addressing future needs.
  - **Examples:** Include plans for medical care, cognitive interventions, and daily support in the care plan.
- **Address Legal and Financial Matters:**
  - **Description:** Take steps to address legal and financial matters, such as establishing power of attorney and making advanced directives.
  - **Examples:** Consult with legal and financial professionals to ensure that all necessary arrangements are in place.

8. Monitor Progress and Adjust

- **Regular Follow-Ups:**
  - **Description:** Schedule regular follow-up appointments with healthcare providers to monitor progress and adjust the care plan as needed.
  - **Examples:** Review cognitive changes and treatment effectiveness during follow-up visits.
- **Reassess Symptoms:**
  - **Description:** Periodically reassess symptoms and their impact to ensure that

interventions are effective and to make any necessary adjustments.

- **Examples:** Update the care plan based on changes in cognitive function and feedback from healthcare professionals.

9. Maintain a Positive Outlook

- **Focus on Strengths:**
    - **Description:** Emphasize and build on cognitive strengths and abilities to maintain a positive outlook and motivation.
    - **Examples:** Engage in activities that highlight and strengthen cognitive abilities, such as hobbies or social interactions.

- **Practice Self-Care:**
    - **Description:** Prioritize self-care and mental well-being to support overall health and resilience.
    - **Examples:** Incorporate relaxation techniques, stress management practices, and healthy lifestyle habits into daily routines.

Professional Help and Therapies Available

When cognitive decline is identified, professional help and therapies can play a crucial role in managing and potentially improving cognitive health. This section provides an overview of various professional resources and therapeutic approaches available for addressing cognitive decline.

1. Healthcare Professionals

- **Primary Care Physicians:**
    - **Role:** Provide initial evaluations, manage overall health, and refer to specialists if needed.
    - **Services:** Conduct preliminary assessments, manage general health conditions, and coordinate care with specialists.
- **Neurologists:**
    - **Role:** Specialize in diagnosing and treating neurological conditions affecting the brain and nervous system.
    - **Services:** Perform detailed neurological evaluations, diagnose conditions such as dementia or Alzheimer's disease, and recommend treatment plans.
- **Geriatricians:**

- - **Role:** Focus on the health care of elderly patients, including managing age-related cognitive decline.
  - **Services:** Conduct comprehensive geriatric assessments, manage multiple health conditions, and provide personalized care plans.
- **Neuropsychologists:**
  - **Role:** Assess cognitive function and provide insights into cognitive deficits and their impact on daily life.
  - **Services:** Perform neuropsychological testing to evaluate memory, attention, language, and other cognitive functions.

2. Diagnostic and Evaluation Tools

- **Neuropsychological Testing:**
  - **Purpose:** Evaluate specific cognitive functions and identify areas of impairment.
  - **Examples:** Tests for memory, attention, executive function, and problem-solving skills.
- **Brain Imaging:**
  - **Purpose:** Detect structural changes in the brain and identify potential causes of cognitive decline.

- **Examples:** MRI (Magnetic Resonance Imaging), CT (Computed Tomography) scans, PET (Positron Emission Tomography) scans.

- **Laboratory Tests:**
    - **Purpose:** Assess for underlying medical conditions or biomarkers that may affect cognitive function.
    - **Examples:** Blood tests to check for vitamin deficiencies, thyroid function, or other metabolic issues.

3. Therapeutic Approaches

- **Medications:**
    - **Purpose:** Manage symptoms or slow the progression of cognitive decline.
    - **Examples:**
        - **Cholinesterase Inhibitors:** Used for Alzheimer's disease to improve symptoms related to memory and thinking (e.g., Donepezil, Rivastigmine).
        - **NMDA Receptor Antagonists:** Used to manage moderate to severe Alzheimer's disease (e.g., Memantine).
- **Cognitive Behavioral Therapy (CBT):**

- - **Purpose:** Address emotional and behavioral issues associated with cognitive decline.
  - **Examples:** Therapy to manage anxiety, depression, or coping with changes in cognitive function.
- **Occupational Therapy:**
  - **Purpose:** Assist individuals in maintaining independence and managing daily activities.
  - **Examples:** Techniques for adapting daily tasks, improving organization, and enhancing quality of life.
- **Speech and Language Therapy:**
  - **Purpose:** Address communication difficulties and improve language skills.
  - **Examples:** Therapy to improve speech, language, and cognitive-communication abilities.

4. Cognitive Rehabilitation Therapy

- **Purpose:** Focus on improving specific cognitive functions through targeted exercises and strategies.
- **Techniques:**
  - **Memory Training:** Exercises to enhance memory recall and retention.

- - **Attention Training:** Activities to improve focus and concentration.
  - **Executive Function Training:** Strategies to enhance problem-solving, planning, and organization.

5. Lifestyle and Behavioral Interventions

- **Health Coaching:**
  - **Purpose:** Support individuals in adopting healthy lifestyle habits that benefit cognitive function.
  - **Examples:** Coaching on diet, exercise, and stress management.
- **Behavioral Interventions:**
  - **Purpose:** Modify behaviors and routines to manage cognitive symptoms and enhance daily functioning.
  - **Examples:** Strategies to manage forgetfulness, improve task organization, and maintain social engagement.

6. Support Services

- **Support Groups:**
  - **Purpose:** Provide emotional support and practical advice for individuals and caregivers.

- - **Examples:** Groups for individuals with cognitive decline, family caregivers, and dementia support groups.

- **Care Management Services:**
  - **Purpose:** Assist in coordinating care, accessing resources, and managing overall care plans.
  - **Examples:** Case managers or care coordinators who help navigate healthcare services and support systems.

7. Research and Clinical Trials

- **Purpose:** Explore new treatments and therapies through ongoing research and clinical trials.

- **Opportunities:**
  - **Participate in Clinical Trials:** Enroll in studies evaluating new medications, therapies, or interventions.
  - **Stay Informed About Research:** Follow advancements in cognitive health research for potential new treatments and strategies.

Chapter 11: Personalized Brain Health Plans

Creating a Personalized Brain Health Action Plan

A Personalized Brain Health Action Plan is essential for tailoring strategies to improve and maintain cognitive function based on individual needs, health conditions, and goals. This chapter provides a structured approach to developing and implementing a customized plan for optimal brain health.

1. Initial Assessment

- **Evaluate Current Cognitive Function:**
    - **Purpose:** Assess baseline cognitive abilities and identify any existing issues.
    - **Actions:**
        - Use cognitive assessments and memory tests.
        - Review medical history and current health conditions.
- **Identify Personal Goals:**
    - **Purpose:** Establish clear objectives for cognitive health and improvement.
    - **Examples:**

- Enhance memory and recall.
- Improve focus and concentration.
- Reduce stress and improve sleep.

2. Tailor Your Nutrition Plan

- **Assess Nutritional Needs:**
  - **Purpose:** Determine dietary requirements that support cognitive health.
  - **Actions:**
    - Consult with a nutritionist or dietitian.
    - Identify and address any nutritional deficiencies.

- **Incorporate Brain-Boosting Foods:**
  - **Purpose:** Support cognitive function through diet.
  - **Examples:**
    - Include foods high in omega-3 fatty acids (e.g., salmon, walnuts).
    - Add antioxidants (e.g., berries, dark leafy greens).
    - Use spices with cognitive benefits (e.g., turmeric, rosemary).

- **Develop a Balanced Meal Plan:**

- **Purpose:** Ensure a diet that supports overall health and cognitive function.
- **Actions:**
  - Plan meals with a focus on balanced nutrition and cognitive-enhancing foods.
  - Monitor dietary intake and make adjustments as needed.

3. Design an Exercise Routine

- **Select Effective Physical Activities:**
  - **Purpose:** Promote cognitive health through regular exercise.
  - **Actions:**
    - Include aerobic exercises (e.g., walking, swimming) for cardiovascular health.
    - Add strength training (e.g., weight lifting) to support physical and cognitive well-being.
    - Incorporate flexibility and balance exercises (e.g., yoga) for overall fitness.
- **Create a Consistent Exercise Schedule:**
  - **Purpose:** Establish a regular exercise routine to support cognitive and physical health.

- **Examples:**
    - Aim for at least 150 minutes of moderate-intensity aerobic activity per week.
    - Include strength training exercises twice a week.

4. Implement Cognitive and Mental Exercises

- **Choose Cognitive Challenges:**
    - **Purpose:** Stimulate and enhance cognitive functions.
    - **Actions:**
        - Engage in puzzles, brain games, and memory exercises.
        - Practice activities that require problem-solving and critical thinking.
- **Promote Lifelong Learning:**
    - **Purpose:** Encourage continuous intellectual engagement.
    - **Examples:**
        - Pursue new hobbies or skills.
        - Participate in educational courses or workshops.

5. Integrate Stress Management Strategies

- **Adopt Stress Reduction Techniques:**

- **Purpose:** Manage stress and support cognitive health.
- **Actions:**
  - Practice mindfulness, meditation, or relaxation techniques.
  - Engage in stress-reducing activities like deep breathing exercises or yoga.

- **Enhance Emotional Well-Being:**
  - **Purpose:** Support mental health to improve cognitive function.
  - **Examples:**
    - Seek therapy or counseling if needed.
    - Participate in activities that promote joy and satisfaction.

6. Prioritize Quality Sleep

- **Develop Healthy Sleep Habits:**
  - **Purpose:** Improve sleep quality to benefit cognitive health.
  - **Actions:**
    - Establish a regular sleep schedule with consistent bedtimes and wake times.

- Create a calming bedtime routine and optimize the sleep environment.
- **Address Sleep Disorders:**
  - **Purpose:** Manage conditions that affect sleep and cognitive function.
  - **Examples:**
    - Consult with a sleep specialist for persistent sleep issues.
    - Explore treatments for sleep disorders like insomnia or sleep apnea.

7. Build and Maintain Social Connections

- **Strengthen Social Engagement:**
  - **Purpose:** Support cognitive health through meaningful social interactions.
  - **Actions:**
    - Participate in social activities, clubs, or community events.
    - Maintain regular contact with family and friends.
- **Engage in Social Activities that Stimulate Cognitive Health:**
  - **Purpose:** Promote mental engagement through social interaction.

- Examples:
  - Join discussion groups or social clubs.
  - Volunteer or participate in group activities that encourage mental stimulation.

8. Monitor and Adjust the Plan

- **Track Progress:**
  - **Purpose:** Evaluate the effectiveness of the action plan and make necessary adjustments.
  - **Actions:**
    - Keep a journal or log to track changes in cognitive function and overall health.
    - Review and assess progress regularly with healthcare professionals.

- **Adjust the Plan as Needed:**
  - **Purpose:** Modify strategies based on progress and evolving needs.
  - **Examples:**
    - Update nutrition, exercise, or cognitive activities as needed.
    - Refine goals and strategies to address new challenges.

9. **Utilize Support Resources**

- **Access Support Services:**
    - **Purpose:** Gain additional resources and support for brain health.
    - **Examples:**
        - Join support groups or networks for individuals with cognitive concerns.
        - Use educational resources and apps designed to support cognitive health.

- **Stay Informed About Research:**
    - **Purpose:** Keep up-to-date with new research and strategies for brain health.
    - **Examples:**
        - Follow credible sources for advancements in cognitive health.
        - Participate in seminars or workshops related to brain health.

Setting Goals and Tracking Progress

Establishing clear goals and systematically tracking progress are crucial steps in improving and maintaining cognitive health. This chapter provides a comprehensive approach to setting achievable goals and monitoring progress to ensure the effectiveness of your brain health plan.

1. Setting SMART Goals

- **Define Specific Goals:**
    - **Purpose:** Clearly articulate what you want to achieve in terms of cognitive health.
    - **Examples:**
        - Improve short-term memory by practicing memory exercises daily.
        - Increase physical activity to enhance cognitive function by completing 30 minutes of exercise, five times a week.

- **Make Goals Measurable:**
    - **Purpose:** Establish criteria to assess progress and success.
    - **Examples:**
        - Track the number of completed cognitive exercises or brain games each week.
        - Measure improvements in cognitive assessments or tests.

- **Ensure Goals are Achievable:**

- **Purpose:** Set realistic and attainable objectives based on current abilities and resources.
- **Examples:**
  - Set incremental goals, such as starting with 10 minutes of exercise and gradually increasing to 30 minutes.
  - Begin with simple cognitive exercises and progress to more challenging activities.

- **Set Relevant Goals:**
  - **Purpose:** Align goals with overall cognitive health and personal priorities.
  - **Examples:**
    - Focus on activities that directly impact cognitive functions, such as memory and concentration.
    - Choose goals that are meaningful and contribute to overall well-being.

- **Establish a Timeline:**
  - **Purpose:** Create deadlines and milestones to stay motivated and on track.
  - **Examples:**

- Set short-term goals with weekly or monthly deadlines.
- Define long-term goals with a timeframe of six months to a year.

2. Developing an Action Plan

- **Create a Step-by-Step Plan:**
    - **Purpose:** Outline specific actions required to achieve each goal.
    - **Actions:**
        - List daily, weekly, and monthly tasks related to each goal.
        - Include resources, tools, or support needed for each step.
- **Incorporate Flexibility:**
    - **Purpose:** Allow for adjustments based on progress and changing circumstances.
    - **Actions:**
        - Review and modify the action plan as needed to accommodate new information or challenges.
        - Adjust goals or strategies based on feedback and results.

3. Tracking Progress

- **Use Tracking Tools:**

- **Purpose:** Monitor progress effectively and stay organized.
- **Tools:**
  - Journals or notebooks to record daily activities and achievements.
  - Digital apps or tools designed for goal tracking and progress monitoring.

- **Record Key Metrics:**
  - **Purpose:** Measure progress towards goals and identify areas for improvement.
  - **Examples:**
    - Track performance on cognitive tests or exercises.
    - Monitor changes in physical health indicators, such as fitness levels or sleep quality.

- **Evaluate Regularly:**
  - **Purpose:** Assess progress and make data-driven decisions.
  - **Actions:**
    - Set regular review dates (e.g., weekly, monthly) to evaluate progress and update goals.

- Analyze trends and patterns to determine effectiveness and areas needing adjustment.

4. Reviewing and Adjusting Goals

- **Assess Achievements:**
    - **Purpose:** Review accomplishments and evaluate goal attainment.
    - **Actions:**
        - Reflect on completed goals and assess their impact on cognitive health.
        - Identify successes and challenges faced during the process.

- **Adjust Goals as Needed:**
    - **Purpose:** Refine goals to better align with evolving needs and priorities.
    - **Examples:**
        - Modify goals based on new insights or changes in cognitive function.
        - Set new goals to address emerging needs or further enhance cognitive health.

- **Celebrate Milestones:**
    - **Purpose:** Acknowledge achievements and stay motivated.

- **Actions:**
  - Reward yourself for reaching milestones or completing significant goals.
  - Reflect on progress and the positive impact on overall well-being.

5. Seeking Support and Feedback

- **Engage Support Systems:**
  - **Purpose:** Utilize support from others to enhance goal achievement.
  - **Actions:**
    - Share goals with family, friends, or support groups for encouragement and accountability.
    - Seek feedback and advice from healthcare professionals or cognitive specialists.

- **Utilize Resources:**
  - **Purpose:** Access additional tools and information to support goal attainment.
  - **Examples:**
    - Use educational resources, apps, or online communities focused on cognitive health.

- Attend workshops or seminars to gain new insights and strategies.

Adapting Your Plan as You Age

As you age, your cognitive and physical needs evolve, requiring adjustments to your brain health plan to maintain and enhance cognitive function. This chapter provides guidance on how to adapt your plan to accommodate the changes that come with aging and ensure continued effectiveness in supporting cognitive health.

1. Understanding Age-Related Changes

- **Recognize Cognitive Changes:**
  - **Purpose:** Identify normal age-related cognitive changes and distinguish them from pathological decline.
  - **Examples:**
    - Mild decline in memory recall or processing speed.
    - Variations in attention span or cognitive flexibility.

- **Acknowledge Physical Changes:**
  - **Purpose:** Understand how physical health changes impact cognitive function.
  - **Examples:**

- Decreased muscle strength and endurance.
- Changes in sensory perception (e.g., vision or hearing).

2. Adjusting Your Nutrition Plan

- **Reassess Nutritional Needs:**
    - **Purpose:** Adapt dietary requirements to support aging-related changes and maintain cognitive health.
    - **Actions:**
        - Consult with a dietitian to address specific age-related nutritional needs.
        - Include foods that support brain health, bone density, and cardiovascular function.

- **Incorporate Age-Appropriate Nutrients:**
    - **Purpose:** Ensure adequate intake of nutrients that support cognitive and overall health.
    - **Examples:**
        - Increase calcium and vitamin D for bone health.
        - Include omega-3 fatty acids to support cognitive function and cardiovascular health.

- **Monitor Dietary Changes:**
  - **Purpose:** Adapt diet to accommodate changes in metabolism and digestion.
  - **Actions:**
    - Adjust portion sizes and meal frequency based on energy levels and appetite.
    - Address any dietary restrictions or preferences that arise with age.

3. Adapting Your Exercise Routine

- **Modify Physical Activities:**
  - **Purpose:** Adjust exercise routines to accommodate changes in strength, flexibility, and endurance.
  - **Actions:**
    - Incorporate low-impact exercises, such as swimming or walking, to reduce joint stress.
    - Add balance and coordination exercises to prevent falls and injuries.
- **Enhance Safety and Accessibility:**
  - **Purpose:** Ensure exercise routines are safe and accessible as physical abilities change.
  - **Examples:**

- Use support equipment or modifications to accommodate physical limitations.
- Choose exercises that can be performed safely at home or with assistance.

- **Monitor and Adjust Intensity:**
    - **Purpose:** Adapt exercise intensity based on physical capabilities and health status.
    - **Actions:**
        - Adjust exercise intensity and duration to match energy levels and physical condition.
        - Incorporate rest and recovery periods as needed.

4. Updating Cognitive and Mental Exercises

- **Choose Age-Appropriate Cognitive Activities:**
    - **Purpose:** Select activities that challenge cognitive abilities while accommodating any changes.
    - **Examples:**
        - Engage in puzzles and brain games that match current cognitive capabilities.

- Explore new hobbies or learning opportunities that stimulate mental engagement.

- **Adjust Difficulty Levels:**
  - **Purpose:** Ensure cognitive exercises remain challenging but achievable.
  - **Actions:**
    - Modify the complexity of cognitive tasks based on performance and comfort level.
    - Introduce new types of mental exercises to maintain interest and engagement.

- **Incorporate Social and Intellectual Activities:**
  - **Purpose:** Support cognitive health through social interaction and intellectual stimulation.
  - **Examples:**
    - Participate in group activities, clubs, or classes.
    - Engage in discussions and activities that encourage mental stimulation.

5. Adapting Stress Management and Emotional Well-Being

- **Update Stress Reduction Techniques:**

- ○ **Purpose:** Adjust stress management strategies to address evolving needs and preferences.
- ○ **Actions:**
  - Explore new relaxation techniques or practices that are enjoyable and effective.
  - Consider adapting stress management strategies based on changing life circumstances.

- **Support Emotional Health:**
  - ○ **Purpose:** Maintain emotional well-being and resilience as life changes.
  - ○ **Examples:**
    - Seek support through counseling or therapy if experiencing significant life transitions.
    - Engage in activities that promote joy, fulfillment, and emotional connection.

6. Revising Sleep Strategies

- **Adjust Sleep Habits:**
  - ○ **Purpose:** Modify sleep routines to address age-related changes in sleep patterns.
  - ○ **Actions:**

- Establish a consistent sleep schedule and create a comfortable sleep environment.
- Address any sleep disturbances or changes in sleep quality.

- **Monitor Sleep Quality:**
  - **Purpose:** Track changes in sleep patterns and their impact on cognitive health.
  - **Examples:**
    - Use sleep tracking tools or consult with a sleep specialist if needed.
    - Make adjustments to bedtime routines or sleep environment as necessary.

7. Strengthening Social Connections

- **Foster Social Engagement:**
  - **Purpose:** Maintain and build social connections to support cognitive and emotional health.
  - **Actions:**
    - Stay connected with family and friends through regular communication and social activities.

- Participate in community events, clubs, or groups that match interests and abilities.

- **Adapt Social Activities:**
    - **Purpose:** Ensure social activities remain enjoyable and accessible.
    - **Examples:**
        - Modify participation in social events based on physical and cognitive capabilities.
        - Explore new social opportunities that align with current interests and abilities.

8. Reviewing and Adjusting Your Plan

- **Regularly Assess and Update:**
    - **Purpose:** Ensure the brain health plan remains effective and relevant.
    - **Actions:**
        - Schedule regular reviews to evaluate progress and make necessary adjustments.
        - Adapt goals and strategies based on changing needs and health status.
- **Celebrate Achievements:**

- **Purpose:** Acknowledge and celebrate progress to maintain motivation and positive outlook.
- **Actions:**
    - Reflect on accomplishments and milestones achieved.
    - Reward yourself for reaching goals and making positive changes.

Chapter 12: Future Directions in Brain Health

Advances in Brain Research and Treatments

Recent developments in brain research and treatments are rapidly expanding our understanding of cognitive health and offering new possibilities for prevention and intervention. This chapter delves into the latest breakthroughs and innovations in brain science and their potential impact on improving and maintaining cognitive function.

1. Neuroscience Breakthroughs

- **Mapping the Brain:**
    - **Purpose:** Explore advancements in brain mapping techniques that enhance our understanding of brain function.
    - **Examples:**
        - **Functional MRI (fMRI):** Improved imaging techniques for visualizing brain activity in real-time.
        - **Connectomics:** Mapping neural connections to understand brain networks and their roles in cognition.

- **Understanding Brain Plasticity:**
  - **Purpose:** Highlight discoveries related to brain plasticity and its implications for cognitive health.
  - **Examples:**
    - **Neurogenesis:** Research on the brain's ability to generate new neurons and its role in learning and memory.
    - **Synaptic Plasticity:** Insights into how synaptic connections strengthen or weaken in response to experiences.

- **Genetic and Epigenetic Research:**
  - **Purpose:** Examine the influence of genetics and epigenetics on brain health and cognitive function.
  - **Examples:**
    - **Genetic Markers:** Identifying genes associated with neurodegenerative diseases and cognitive decline.
    - **Epigenetic Modifications:** Understanding how environmental factors and lifestyle choices affect gene expression related to brain health.

2. Innovations in Brain Treatments

- **Pharmacological Advances:**
  - **Purpose:** Explore new medications and drug therapies for cognitive health and neurodegenerative diseases.
  - **Examples:**
    - **Disease-Modifying Drugs:** Research on drugs that target the underlying pathology of conditions like Alzheimer's disease.
    - **Cognitive Enhancers:** Development of medications aimed at improving cognitive function and memory.

- **Gene Therapy:**
  - **Purpose:** Discuss the potential of gene therapy for treating or preventing brain disorders.
  - **Examples:**
    - **Gene Editing:** Techniques like CRISPR for modifying genes associated with neurodegenerative diseases.
    - **Gene Replacement:** Strategies for introducing or correcting genes to address genetic deficits.

- **Neurostimulation Techniques:**

- **Purpose:** Highlight advances in neurostimulation methods for modulating brain activity.
- **Examples:**
  - **Transcranial Magnetic Stimulation (TMS):** Non-invasive technique that uses magnetic fields to stimulate specific brain regions.
  - **Deep Brain Stimulation (DBS):** Implantable devices that deliver electrical impulses to targeted brain areas to treat movement disorders and depression.

3. Cutting-Edge Brain Imaging and Diagnostics

- **Advanced Imaging Techniques:**
  - **Purpose:** Review the latest imaging technologies for studying brain structure and function.
  - **Examples:**
    - **PET Scans:** Use of positron emission tomography to detect biochemical changes in the brain.
    - **Magnetoencephalography (MEG):** Techniques for measuring magnetic fields produced by brain activity.
- **Biomarkers and Diagnostics:**

- **Purpose:** Explore the role of biomarkers in diagnosing and monitoring brain health.
- **Examples:**
  - **Biomarker Identification:** Discovery of biological markers associated with early stages of cognitive decline.
  - **Diagnostic Tests:** Development of tests for early detection and assessment of brain disorders.

4. Personalized Medicine in Brain Health

- **Tailored Treatments:**
  - **Purpose:** Discuss the shift towards personalized approaches in brain health management.
  - **Examples:**
    - **Personalized Drug Therapy:** Customizing medication based on genetic profiles and individual responses.
    - **Precision Nutrition:** Developing dietary recommendations based on genetic and metabolic profiles.
- **Individualized Interventions:**
  - **Purpose:** Highlight strategies for creating personalized cognitive health plans.

- Examples:
  - **Customized Cognitive Training:** Designing brain training programs tailored to individual needs and abilities.
  - **Behavioral and Lifestyle Modifications:** Personalizing lifestyle changes to address specific risk factors and health goals.

5. Future Directions in Brain Research

- **Integration of Multidisciplinary Approaches:**
  - **Purpose:** Emphasize the importance of combining insights from various fields in brain research.
  - **Examples:**
    - **Collaborative Research:** Integration of neuroscience, psychology, genetics, and technology to address complex brain health issues.
    - **Holistic Models:** Developing comprehensive models that incorporate biological, psychological, and social factors.
- **Long-Term Studies and Clinical Trials:**

- **Purpose:** Address the need for extensive research to understand long-term effects and efficacy of treatments.
- **Examples:**
  - **Longitudinal Research:** Studies tracking cognitive health over extended periods to identify patterns and outcomes.
  - **Innovative Clinical Trials:** Trials testing new therapies and interventions with robust methodologies and diverse participant groups.

- **Ethical and Social Considerations:**
  - **Purpose:** Explore ethical issues related to advancements in brain research and treatments.
  - **Examples:**
    - **Ethics of Genetic Manipulation:** Considerations surrounding gene editing and its implications for individuals and society.
    - **Access and Equity:** Addressing disparities in access to advanced treatments and technologies.

Promising Therapies and Interventions

As the field of brain health continues to advance, new therapies and interventions are emerging that offer hope for improving cognitive function, preventing decline, and treating neurodegenerative diseases. This chapter explores some of the most promising therapies and interventions currently being researched or implemented.

1. Pharmacological Therapies

- **Novel Drug Development:**
    - **Purpose:** Review new medications designed to treat or prevent cognitive decline and neurodegenerative diseases.
    - **Examples:**
        - **Anti-Amyloid Drugs:** Medications targeting amyloid plaques in Alzheimer's disease.
        - **Neuroprotective Agents:** Drugs designed to protect brain cells from damage and degeneration.
- **Cognitive Enhancers:**
    - **Purpose:** Explore drugs aimed at improving cognitive function in individuals with and without cognitive impairments.

- Examples:
  - **Cholinesterase Inhibitors:** Medications that increase levels of acetylcholine, a neurotransmitter important for memory and learning.
  - **Nootropics:** Compounds that may enhance cognitive performance and mental clarity.

- **Personalized Pharmacotherapy:**
  - **Purpose:** Discuss the trend towards customizing drug treatments based on individual genetic profiles and health conditions.
  - Examples:
    - **Genetic Testing:** Using genetic information to guide medication choices and dosages.
    - **Tailored Drug Regimens:** Adjusting drug therapies to individual responses and side effects.

2. Gene Therapy

- **Gene Editing Techniques:**
  - **Purpose:** Explore the use of gene editing technologies to address genetic causes of cognitive disorders.

- Examples:
  - **CRISPR-Cas9:** A revolutionary technique for editing genes associated with neurodegenerative diseases.
  - **Gene Insertion:** Introducing new or modified genes to correct genetic defects.

- **Gene Therapy Applications:**
  - **Purpose:** Highlight practical applications of gene therapy in treating brain disorders.
  - Examples:
    - **Treatment for Rare Genetic Disorders:** Using gene therapy to address conditions like Huntington's disease.
    - **Restoring Gene Function:** Approaches to correct or replace malfunctioning genes linked to cognitive decline.

3. Neurostimulation and Neuromodulation

- **Transcranial Magnetic Stimulation (TMS):**
  - **Purpose:** Examine TMS as a non-invasive technique for modulating brain activity and treating cognitive disorders.
  - Examples:

- **Depression Treatment:** Using TMS to improve symptoms of depression and enhance cognitive function.
- **Rehabilitation:** Employing TMS for cognitive rehabilitation following brain injury or stroke.

- **Deep Brain Stimulation (DBS):**
  - **Purpose:** Discuss the use of DBS to treat various neurological and psychiatric conditions.
  - **Examples:**
    - **Movement Disorders:** Using DBS to manage symptoms of Parkinson's disease and essential tremor.
    - **Cognitive Enhancement:** Research into DBS for enhancing cognitive function and memory.

- **Vagus Nerve Stimulation (VNS):**
  - **Purpose:** Explore VNS as a method to influence brain function through stimulation of the vagus nerve.
  - **Examples:**
    - **Epilepsy Treatment:** Using VNS to reduce seizure frequency in epilepsy patients.

- **Mood Disorders:** Investigating VNS for treating mood disorders and improving cognitive health.

4. Cognitive and Behavioral Therapies

- **Cognitive Training Programs:**
    - **Purpose:** Review interventions designed to enhance cognitive abilities through structured training.
    - **Examples:**
        - **Memory Training:** Programs focused on improving memory recall and retention.
        - **Attention and Processing Speed:** Training exercises aimed at enhancing attention and cognitive processing speed.
- **Behavioral Interventions:**
    - **Purpose:** Discuss therapeutic approaches that address behavioral and emotional aspects of cognitive health.
    - **Examples:**
        - **Cognitive Behavioral Therapy (CBT):** Techniques for managing cognitive and emotional symptoms.
        - **Behavioral Activation:** Strategies for increasing engagement in

activities that promote cognitive well-being.

- **Mindfulness and Meditation:**
    - **Purpose:** Examine the impact of mindfulness and meditation practices on cognitive health.
    - **Examples:**
        - **Mindfulness-Based Stress Reduction (MBSR):** Techniques for reducing stress and enhancing cognitive function.
        - **Meditation Practices:** Exploring various meditation methods for improving focus and mental clarity.

5. Lifestyle and Environmental Interventions

- **Nutritional Interventions:**
    - **Purpose:** Highlight dietary strategies and supplements that support brain health.
    - **Examples:**
        - **Diets Rich in Antioxidants:** Incorporating foods high in antioxidants to protect brain cells from oxidative stress.
        - **Supplementation:** Using supplements like omega-3 fatty

acids and B vitamins to support cognitive function.

- **Physical Activity:**
  - **Purpose:** Discuss the role of exercise in maintaining and improving cognitive health.
  - **Examples:**
    - **Aerobic Exercise:** Benefits of regular aerobic exercise for brain health and cognitive performance.
    - **Strength Training:** Impact of resistance training on cognitive function and overall brain health.

- **Social and Environmental Enrichment:**
  - **Purpose:** Explore how social interactions and environmental factors influence cognitive health.
  - **Examples:**
    - **Social Engagement:** Importance of maintaining social connections and participating in community activities.
    - **Enriched Environments:** Creating stimulating environments that encourage cognitive engagement and learning.

6. Future Prospects and Research Directions

- **Emerging Therapies:**
  - **Purpose:** Highlight promising new therapies and interventions currently under investigation.
  - **Examples:**
    - **Stem Cell Therapy:** Research into using stem cells for repairing and regenerating brain tissue.
    - **Biological Treatments:** Developing treatments based on biological markers and pathways involved in cognitive decline.
- **Integration of Technology:**
  - **Purpose:** Explore how technology is enhancing brain health interventions.
  - **Examples:**
    - **Virtual Reality (VR):** Using VR for cognitive training and rehabilitation.
    - **Wearable Devices:** Monitoring and enhancing brain health through wearable technology.
- **Personalized Approaches:**
  - **Purpose:** Discuss the trend towards personalized medicine and individualized interventions.

- **Examples:**
  - **Genomic Insights:** Using genetic information to tailor treatments and prevention strategies.
  - **Customized Programs:** Developing personalized cognitive health plans based on individual needs and responses.

The Future of Cognitive Health and Longevity

As our understanding of cognitive health and longevity evolves, the future promises exciting advancements in science, technology, and personalized care. This chapter explores the emerging trends, innovations, and future directions shaping the future of cognitive health and how they might impact our ability to maintain cognitive function and longevity.

1. Advances in Neuroscience and Cognitive Research

- **Cutting-Edge Brain Research:**
  - **Purpose:** Highlight the latest breakthroughs in neuroscience and their implications for cognitive health.
  - **Examples:**
    - **Neurogenesis Research:** Ongoing studies into the brain's ability to create new neurons and its

potential for cognitive enhancement.

- **Brain Connectivity Mapping:** Innovations in mapping brain networks to better understand how different regions communicate and function.

- Genetic and Epigenetic Discoveries:
  - **Purpose:** Examine advances in genetics and epigenetics that could influence cognitive health.
  - **Examples:**
    - **Gene Therapy:** New approaches to correcting genetic mutations linked to cognitive disorders.
    - **Epigenetic Modulation:** Strategies to modify gene expression related to brain health through lifestyle and environmental factors.

2. Emerging Technologies in Brain Health
- Artificial Intelligence (AI) and Machine Learning:
  - **Purpose:** Explore how AI and machine learning are transforming cognitive health research and care.
  - **Examples:**

- **Predictive Analytics:** Using AI to predict cognitive decline and personalize interventions.
- **Data-Driven Insights:** Analyzing large datasets to uncover patterns and new approaches in brain health.

- **Wearable and Implantable Technologies:**
  - **Purpose:** Discuss the role of wearable and implantable devices in monitoring and improving cognitive function.
  - **Examples:**
    - **Smart Wearables:** Devices that track brain activity, sleep, and cognitive performance in real-time.
    - **Neuroimplants:** Innovations in implantable devices for continuous monitoring and stimulation of brain areas.

- **Virtual Reality (VR) and Augmented Reality (AR):**
  - **Purpose:** Investigate the use of VR and AR technologies for cognitive training and rehabilitation.
  - **Examples:**
    - **VR Cognitive Training:** Immersive environments designed

to enhance memory, attention, and other cognitive skills.

- **AR for Daily Life:** Augmented reality applications that support cognitive tasks and improve interaction with the environment.

3. Personalized Medicine and Tailored Interventions

- **Precision Health Approaches:**
  - **Purpose:** Explore the shift towards personalized and precision medicine in cognitive health.
  - **Examples:**
    - **Genetic Profiling:** Using genetic information to tailor interventions and treatments.
    - **Customized Health Plans:** Developing individualized cognitive health strategies based on personal risk factors and needs.
- **Biomarker-Based Diagnostics:**
  - **Purpose:** Highlight the role of biomarkers in diagnosing and monitoring cognitive health.
  - **Examples:**

- **Early Detection Biomarkers:** Identifying biomarkers that signal early cognitive decline.

- **Personalized Monitoring:** Using biomarkers to customize health interventions and track progress.

4. Innovative Preventive Strategies

- **Lifestyle and Environmental Interventions:**
  - **Purpose:** Discuss new strategies for maintaining cognitive health through lifestyle and environmental changes.
  - **Examples:**
    - **Dietary Innovations:** Emerging research on diets that promote brain health and longevity.
    - **Environmental Enrichment:** Creating stimulating environments that support cognitive engagement and prevent decline.

- **Behavioral and Social Interventions:**
  - **Purpose:** Explore innovative approaches to behavioral and social aspects of cognitive health.
  - **Examples:**
    - **Social Engagement Programs:** Initiatives designed to enhance

social connections and cognitive stimulation.

- **Mental and Emotional Health:** Integrating mental health practices and emotional well-being into cognitive health strategies.

5. The Role of Public Health and Policy

- **Global Health Initiatives:**
  - **Purpose:** Examine global efforts and public health policies aimed at promoting cognitive health.
  - **Examples:**
    - **Public Awareness Campaigns:** Programs to increase awareness and education about cognitive health.
    - **Health Policy Changes:** Policy developments that support research, funding, and access to cognitive health resources.

- **Aging Populations and Societal Impact:**
  - **Purpose:** Address the challenges and opportunities related to aging populations and cognitive health.
  - **Examples:**
    - **Age-Friendly Communities:** Creating environments that

support cognitive health in older adults.

- **Long-Term Care Innovations:** Developing new models for long-term care that prioritize cognitive health and quality of life.

6. Ethical and Social Considerations

- **Ethical Implications of New Technologies:**
    - **Purpose:** Discuss the ethical issues surrounding new technologies and interventions in cognitive health.
    - **Examples:**
        - **Privacy Concerns:** Ensuring data security and privacy in the use of wearable and implantable devices.
        - **Access and Equity:** Addressing disparities in access to advanced technologies and personalized care.

- **Societal Impact and Acceptance:**
    - **Purpose:** Explore the societal impact of advancements in cognitive health and their acceptance.
    - **Examples:**
        - **Public Perception:** Understanding how new

interventions and technologies are received by the public.

- **Societal Norms:** Evaluating how cultural and societal norms influence the adoption of cognitive health innovations.

7. Future Research and Exploration

- **Emerging Research Areas:**
  - **Purpose:** Highlight potential future research directions in cognitive health.
  - **Examples:**
    - **Neurotherapeutics:** Exploring novel therapeutic approaches for brain health.
    - **Interdisciplinary Collaboration:** Promoting collaboration between neuroscience, technology, and public health.

- **Innovative Study Designs:**
  - **Purpose:** Discuss innovative approaches to studying cognitive health and longevity.
  - **Examples:**
    - **Longitudinal Studies:** Research tracking cognitive health over extended periods to identify effective interventions.

- **Experimental Models:** Developing new experimental models to test theories and treatments for cognitive decline.

Conclusion

As we reach the end of our exploration into cognitive health and longevity, it is essential to reflect on the key insights and actionable strategies presented throughout the book. The journey through understanding cognitive health, the science behind neuroplasticity, the importance of nutrition, exercise, mental stimulation, and other critical factors provides a holistic view of how to maintain and enhance cognitive function throughout life.

1. Recap of Key Points

- **Understanding Cognitive Health:**
    - We have delved into the fundamental aspects of cognitive health, including brain anatomy, aging, and the causes of cognitive decline. Recognizing the signs and factors contributing to cognitive health is the first step toward effective prevention and management.

- **The Science of Neuroplasticity:**
    - Neuroplasticity has emerged as a central theme, demonstrating the brain's remarkable ability to adapt and reorganize itself. Harnessing neuroplasticity through targeted exercises and interventions can play a crucial role in cognitive enhancement and recovery.

- **Nutrition and Brain Health:**
    - The impact of nutrition on cognitive function has been highlighted, emphasizing the importance of a balanced diet rich in essential nutrients. Specific brain-boosting foods and dietary strategies have been discussed to support cognitive health.

- **Exercise and Brain Function:**
    - The relationship between physical exercise and cognitive health has been explored, revealing how regular physical activity can positively influence brain function and protect against cognitive decline.

- **Mental Exercises and Cognitive Training:**
    - Engaging in mental exercises and cognitive training activities has been shown to enhance memory, focus, and overall cognitive performance. Puzzles, games, and continuous learning are valuable tools for maintaining brain health.

- **Stress Management and Sleep:**
    - Effective stress management and quality sleep are critical for optimal cognitive function. Techniques for reducing stress and improving sleep have been discussed

as integral components of a brain health strategy.

- **Social Connections and Technology:**
  - The role of social interaction and the impact of technology on cognitive health have been addressed. Building strong social networks and balancing technology use are essential for cognitive engagement and well-being.

- **Future Directions and Innovations:**
  - Looking ahead, advancements in research, technology, and personalized medicine offer promising avenues for improving cognitive health. Emerging therapies, innovative interventions, and ongoing research hold the potential for significant progress in brain health.

2. Emphasizing the Importance of a Holistic Approach

Maintaining cognitive health is not a single-faceted endeavor but requires a comprehensive, holistic approach. It involves integrating various aspects of lifestyle, including diet, exercise, mental stimulation, stress management, and social engagement. Adopting a balanced and proactive approach to these elements can contribute to a healthier, more resilient brain.

3. Encouragement for Lifelong Commitment

Improving and maintaining cognitive health is a lifelong commitment. It requires dedication to adopting and sustaining healthy habits and being proactive about managing cognitive risks. By integrating the strategies discussed in this book into daily life, individuals can take charge of their cognitive well-being and enhance their quality of life.

4. Call to Action

- **Implement Strategies:** Encourage readers to start incorporating the actionable strategies from the book into their daily routines. Small, consistent changes can lead to significant improvements in cognitive health.

- **Stay Informed:** Remind readers to stay informed about the latest research and advancements in cognitive health. Continuous learning and adaptation are key to staying ahead in maintaining cognitive function.

- **Seek Professional Guidance:** Advise readers to consult with healthcare professionals for personalized advice and support. Professional guidance can help tailor strategies to individual needs and ensure optimal outcomes.

5. Final Thoughts

Cognitive health and longevity are achievable goals with the right knowledge and commitment. By understanding the factors that influence brain health and actively engaging in practices that support cognitive function, individuals can foster a healthier, more vibrant life. The journey to better cognitive health is ongoing, and the tools and insights provided in this book serve as a foundation for lifelong well-being.

Made in United States
North Haven, CT
19 September 2024